MTEL ESL 54

MTEL English as a Second Language (ESL)
Teacher Certification Exam

By: Sharon Wynne, M.S.

BICS
basic interpersonal communication skills

CALP
Cognitive academic language proficiency

Cummins

XAMonline, INC.
Boston

XAMonline, Inc.
25 First Street, Suite 106
Cambridge, MA 02141
Toll Free 1-800-509-4128
Email: info@xamonline.com
Web: www.xamonline.com
Fax: 1-617-583-5552

Library of Congress Cataloging-in-Publication Data
Wynne, Sharon A.
MTEL English as a Second Language (ESL) 54 Teacher Certification / Sharon A. Wynne.
  ISBN: 978-1-60787-084-5, 1st edition
1. MTEL English as a Second Language (ESL) 54 2. Study Guides. 3. MTEL
4. Teachers' Certification & Licensure. 5. Careers

Disclaimer:
The opinions expressed in this publication are the sole works of XAMonline and were created independently from the National Education Association (NES), Educational Testing Service (ETS), or any State Department of Education, National Evaluation Systems or other testing affiliates. Between the time of publication and printing, state specific standards as well as testing formats and website information may change that are not included in part or in whole within this product. XAMonline develops sample test questions, and they reflect similar content as on real tests; however, they are not former tests. XAMonline assembles content that aligns with state standards but makes no claims nor guarantees teacher candidates a passing score. Numerical scores are determined by testing companies such as NES or ETS and then are compared with individual state standards. A passing score varies from state to state.

Printed in the United States of America   œ-1
MTEL English as a Second Language (ESL) 54
ISBN: 978-1-60787-084-5

TABLE OF CONTENTS

Section 1 About XAMonline

XAMonline – A Specialty Teacher Certification Company

Created in 1996, XAMonline was the first company to publish study guides for state-specific teacher certification examinations. Founder Sharon Wynne found it frustrating that materials were not available for teacher certification preparation and decided to create the first single, state-specific guide. XAMonline has grown into a company of over 1800 contributors and writers and offers over 300 titles for the entire PRAXIS series and every state examination. No matter what state you plan on teaching in, XAMonline has a unique teacher certification study guide just for you.

XAMonline – Value and Innovation

We are committed to providing value and innovation. Our print-on-demand technology allows us to be the first in the market to reflect changes in test standards and user feedback as they occur. Our guides are written by experienced teachers who are experts in their fields. And, our content reflects the highest standards of quality. Comprehensive practice tests with varied levels of rigor means that your study experience will closely match the actual in-test experience.

To date, XAMonline has helped nearly 600,000 teachers pass their certification or licensing exams. Our commitment to preparation exceeds simply providing the proper material for study - it extends to helping teachers **gain mastery** of the subject matter, giving them the **tools** to become the most effective classroom leaders possible, and ushering today's students toward a **successful future**.

Section 2 About this Study Guide

Purpose of this Guide

Is there a little voice inside of you saying, "Am I ready?" Our goal is to replace that little voice and remove all doubt with a new voice that says, "I AM READY. **Bring it on**!" by offering the highest quality of teacher certification study guides.

Organization of Content

You will see that while every test may start with overlapping general topics, each are very unique in the skills they wish to test. Only XAMonline presents custom content that analyzes deeper than a title, a subarea, or an objective. Only XAMonline presents content and sample test assessments along with **focus statements**, the deepest-level rationale and interpretation of the skills that are unique to the exam.

Title and field number of test

→Each exam has its own name and number. XAMonline's guides are written to give you the content you need to know for the specific exam you are taking. You can be confident when you buy our guide that it contains the information you need to study for the specific test you are taking.

Subareas

→These are the major content categories found on the exam. XAMonline's guides are written to cover all of the subareas found in the test frameworks developed for the exam.

Objectives

→These are standards that are unique to the exam and represent the main subcategories of the subareas/content categories. XAMonline's guides are written to address every specific objective required to pass the exam.

Focus statements

→These are examples and interpretations of the objectives. You find them in parenthesis directly following the objective. They provide detailed examples of the range, type, and level of content that appear on the test questions. **Only XAMonline's guides drill down to this level.**

How do We Compare with Our Competitors?

XAMonline – drills down to the focus statement level
CliffsNotes and REA – organized at the objective level
Kaplan – provides only links to content
MoMedia – content not specific to the test

Each subarea is divided into manageable sections that cover the specific skill areas. Explanations are easy-to-understand and thorough. You'll find that every test answer contains a rejoinder so if you need a refresher or further review after taking the test, you'll know exactly to which section you must return.

How to Use this Book

Our informal polls show that most people begin studying up to 8 weeks prior to the test date, so start early. Then ask yourself some questions: How much do you really know? Are you coming to the test straight from your teacher-education program or are you having to review subjects you haven't considered in 10 years? Either way, take a **diagnostic or assessment test** first. Also, spend time on sample tests so that you become accustomed to the way the actual test will appear.

This guide comes with an online diagnostic test of 30 questions found online at www.XAMonline.com. It is a little boot camp to get you up for the task and reveal things about your compendium of knowledge in general. Although this guide is structured to follow the order of the test, you are not required to study in that order. By finding a time-management and study plan that fits your life you will be more effective. The results of your diagnostic or self-assessment test can be a guide for how to manage your time and point you towards an area that needs more attention.

Week	Activity
8 weeks prior to test	Take a diagnostic test found at www.XAMonline.com
6-3 weeks prior to test	For each of these 4 weeks, choose a content area to study. You don't have to go in the order of the book. It may be that you start with the content that needs the most review. Alternately, you may want to ease yourself into plan by starting with the most familiar material.
2 weeks prior to test	Take the sample test, score it, and create a review plan for the final week before the test.
1 week prior to test	Following your plan (which will likely be aligned with the areas that need the most review) go back and study the sections that align with the questions you may have gotten wrong. Then go back and study the sections related to the questions you answered correctly. If need be, create flashcards and drill yourself on any area that you makes you anxious.

Section 3 About the MTEL English as a Second Language (ESL) 54

What is the MTEL English as a Second Language (ESL) 54?
The MTEL English as a Second Language (ESL) 54 exam is meant to assess mastery of the basic pedagogical knowledge and skills required to teach ELL students in Massachusetts public schools. It is administered by Pearson Education on behalf of the Massachusetts Department of Education.

Often **your own state's requirements** determine whether or not you should take any particular test. The most reliable source of information regarding this is your state's Department of Education. This resource should have a complete list of testing centers and dates. Test dates vary by subject area and not all test dates necessarily include your particular test, so be sure to check carefully.

If you are in a teacher-education program, check with the Education Department or the Certification Officer for specific information for testing and testing timelines. The Certification Office should have most of the information you need.

If you choose an alternative route to certification you can either rely on our website at www.XAMonline.com or on the resources provided by an alternative certification program. Many states now have specific agencies devoted to alternative certification and there are some national organizations as well, for example:
National Association for Alternative Certification
http://www.alt-teachercert.org/index.asp

Interpreting Test Results
Contrary to what you may have heard, the results of the MTEL English as a Second Language (ESL) 54 are not based on time. More accurately, you will be scored on the raw number of points you earn in relation to the raw number of points available. Each question is worth one raw point. It is likely to your benefit to complete as many questions in the time allotted, but it will not necessarily work to your advantage if you hurry through the test.

Follow the guidelines provided by Pearson for interpreting your score. The web site offers a sample test score sheet and clearly explains how/whether the scores are scaled and what to expect if you have an essay portion on your test.

What's on the Test?
The MTEL English as a Second Language (ESL) 54 consists of approximately 100 multiple-choice questions and 4 constructed-response essays. The breakdown of the questions is as follows:

Category	Question Type	Approximate Percentage of the test
I: English Language Listening Proficiency	Multiple choice	10%
II: Foundations of Second Language Instruction	Multiple choice	25%
III: Second Language and Content Learning	Multiple choice	45%
IV: English Language Oral Proficiency	Constructed response	20%

Question Types

You're probably thinking, enough already, I want to study! Indulge us a little longer while we explain that there is actually more than one type of multiple-choice question. You can thank us later after you realize how well prepared you are for your exam.

1. **Complete the Statement**. The name says it all. In this question type you'll be asked to choose the correct completion of a given statement. For example: The Dolch Basic Sight Words consist of a relatively short list of words that children should be able to:
    a. Sound out
    b. Know the meaning of
    c. Recognize on sight
    d. Use in a sentence

   The correct answer is C. In order to check your answer, test out the statement by adding the choices to the end of it.

2. **Which of the Following**. One way to test your answer choice for this type of question is to replace the phrase "which of the following" with your selection. Use this example: Which of the following words is one of the twelve most frequently used in children's reading texts:
    a. There
    b. This
    c. The
    d. An

   Don't look! Test your answer. _____ is one of the twelve most frequently used in children's reading texts. Did you guess C? Then you guessed correctly.

3. **Roman Numeral Choices**. This question type is used when there is more than one possible correct answer. For example: Which of the following two arguments accurately supports the use of cooperative learning as an effective method of instruction?
    I. Cooperative learning groups facilitate healthy competition between individuals in the group.
    II. Cooperative learning groups allow academic achievers to carry or cover for academic underachievers.
    III. Cooperative learning groups make each student in the group accountable for the success of the group.
    IV. Cooperative learning groups make it possible for students to reward other group members for achieving.
        A. I and II
        B. II and III
        C. I and III
        D. III and IV

   Notice that the question states there are **two** possible answers. It's best to read all the possibilities first before looking at the answer choices. In this case, the correct answer is D.

4. **Negative Questions**. This type of question contains words such as "not," "least," and "except." Each correct answer will be the statement that does not fit the situation described in the question. Such as: Multicultural education is not

   a. An idea or concept
   b. A "tack-on" to the school curriculum
   c. An educational reform movement
   d. A process

Think to yourself that the statement could be anything but the correct answer. This question form is more open to interpretation than other types, so read carefully and don't forget that you're answering a negative statement.

5. **Questions That Include Graphs, Tables, or Reading Passages**. As ever, read the question carefully. It likely asks for a very specific answer and not broad interpretation of the visual. Here is a simple (though not statistically accurate) example of a graph question: In the following graph in how many years did more men take the NYSTCE exam than women?

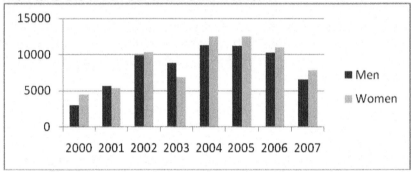

   a. None
   b. One
   c. Two
   d. Three

It may help you to simply circle the two years that answer the question. Make sure you've read the question thoroughly and once you've made your determination, double check your work. The correct answer is C.

Section 4 Helpful Hints

Study Tips

1. **You are what you eat**. Certain foods aid the learning process by releasing natural memory enhancers called CCKs (cholecystokinin) composed of tryptophan, choline, and phenylalanine. All of these chemicals enhance the neurotransmitters associated with memory and certain foods release memory enhancing chemicals. A light meal or snacks from the following foods fall into this category:

   - Milk
   - Nuts and seeds
   - Rice
   - Oats
   - Eggs
   - Turkey
   - Fish

   The better the connections, the more you comprehend!

2. **See the forest for the trees**. In other words, get the concept before you look at the details. One way to do this is to take notes as you read, paraphrasing or summarizing in your own words. Putting the concept in terms that are comfortable and familiar may increase retention.

3. **Question authority**. Ask why, why, why. Pull apart written material paragraph by paragraph and don't forget the captions under the illustrations. For example, if a heading reads *Stream Erosion* put it in the form of a question (why do streams erode? Or what is stream erosion?) then find the answer within the material. If you train your mind to think in this manner you will learn more and prepare yourself for answering test questions.

4. **Play mind games**. Using your brain for reading or puzzles keeps it flexible. Even with a limited amount of time your brain can take in data (much like a computer) and store it for later use. In ten minutes you can: read two paragraphs (at least), quiz yourself with flash cards, or review notes. Even if you don't fully understand something on the first pass, your mind stores it for recall, which is why frequent reading or review increases chances of retention and comprehension.

5. **The pen is mightier than the sword**. Learn to take great notes. A by-product of our modern culture is that we have grown accustomed to getting our information in short doses. We've subconsciously trained ourselves to assimilate information into neat little packages. Messy notes fragment the flow of information. Your notes can be much clearer with proper formatting. *The Cornell Method* is one such format. This method was popularized in *How to Study in College,* Ninth Edition, by Walter Pauk. You can benefit from the method without purchasing an additional book by simply looking the method up online. Below is a sample of how *The Cornell Method* can be adapted for use with this guide.

← 2 ½" →	← —————————————— 6" —————————————— →
Cue Column	Note Taking Column
	1. Record: During your reading, use the note-taking column to record important points.
	2. Questions: As soon as you finish a section, formulate questions based on the notes in the right-hand column. Writing questions helps to clarify meanings, reveal relationships, establish community, and strengthen memory. Also, the writing of questions sets the state for exam study later.
	3. Recite: Cover the note-taking column with a sheet of paper. Then, looking at the questions or cue-words in the question and cue column only, say aloud, in your own words, the answers to the questions, facts, or ideas indicated by the cue words.
	4. Reflect: Reflect on the material by asking yourself questions.
	5. Review: Spend at least ten minutes every week reviewing all your previous notes. Doing so helps you retain ideas and topics for the exam.
↑ 2" ↓	Summary
	After reading, use this space to summarize the notes from each page.

*Adapted from *How to Study in College,* Ninth Edition, by Walter Pauk, ©2008 Wadsworth

6. **Place yourself in exile and set the mood**. Set aside a particular place and time to study that best suits your personal needs and biorhythms. If you're a night person, burn the midnight oil. If you're a morning person set yourself up with some coffee and get to it. Make your study time and place as free from distraction as possible and surround yourself with what you need, be it silence or music. Studies have shown that music can aid in concentration, absorption, and retrieval of information. Not all music, though. Classical music is said to work best.

7. **Get pointed in the right direction**. Use arrows to point to important passages or pieces of information. It's easier to read than a page full of yellow highlights. Highlighting can be used sparingly, but add an arrow to the margin to call attention to it.

8. **Check your budget**. You should at least review all the content material before your test, but allocate the most amount of time to the areas that need the most refreshing. It sounds obvious, but it's easy to forget. You can use the study rubric above to balance your study budget.

The proctor will write the start time where it can be seen and then, later, provide the time remaining, typically 15 minutes before the end of the test

Testing Tips

1. **Get smart, play dumb**. Sometimes a question is just a question. No one is out to trick you, so don't assume that the test writer is looking for something other than what was asked. Stick to the question as written and don't overanalyze.

2. **Do a double take**. Read test questions and answer choices at least twice because it's easy to miss something, to transpose a word or some letters. If you have no idea what the correct answer is, skip it and come back later if there's time. If you're still clueless, it's okay to guess. Remember, you're scored on the number of questions you answer correctly and you're not penalized for wrong answers. The worst case scenario is that you miss a point from a good guess.

3. **Turn it on its ear**. The syntax of a question can often provide a clue, so make things interesting and turn the question into a statement to see if it changes the meaning or relates better (or worse) to the answer choices.

4. **Get out your magnifying glass**. Look for hidden clues in the questions because it's difficult to write a multiple-choice question without giving away part of the answer in the options presented. In most questions you can readily eliminate one or two potential answers, increasing your chances of answering correctly to 50/50, which will help out if you've skipped a question and gone back to it (see tip #2).

5. **Call it intuition**. Often your first instinct is correct. If you've been studying the content you've likely absorbed something and have subconsciously retained the knowledge. On questions you're not sure about trust your instincts because a first impression is usually correct.

6. **Graffiti**. Sometimes it's a good idea to mark your answers directly on the test booklet and go back to fill in the optical scan sheet later. You don't get extra points for perfectly blackened ovals. If you choose to manage your test this way, be sure not to mismark your answers when you transcribe to the scan sheet.

7. **Become a clock-watcher**. You have a set amount of time to answer the questions. Don't get bogged down laboring over a question you're not sure about when there are ten others you could answer more readily. If you choose to follow the advice of tip #6, be sure you leave time near the end to go back and fill in the scan sheet.

Do the Drill

No matter how prepared you feel it's sometimes a good idea to apply Murphy's Law. So the following tips might seem silly, mundane, or obvious, but we're including them anyway.

1. **Remember, you are what you eat, so bring a snack**. Choose from the list of energizing foods that appear earlier in the introduction.

2. **You're not too sexy for your test**. Wear comfortable clothes. You'll be distracted if your belt is too tight, or if you're too cold or too hot.

3. **Lie to yourself**. Even if you think you're a prompt person, pretend you're not and leave plenty of time to get to the testing center. Map it out ahead of time and do a dry run if you have to. There's no need to add road rage to your list of anxieties.

4. **Bring sharp, number 2 pencils**. It may seem impossible to forget this need from your school days, but you might. And make sure the erasers are intact, too.

5. **No ticket, no test**. Bring your admission ticket as well as two forms of identification, including one with a picture and signature. You will not be admitted to the test without these things.

6. **You can't take it with you**. Leave any study aids, dictionaries, notebooks, computers and the like at home. Certain tests do allow a scientific or four-function calculator, so check ahead of time if your test does.

7. **Prepare for the desert**. Any time spent on a bathroom break cannot be made up later, so use your judgment on the amount you eat or drink.

8. **Quiet, Please!** Keeping your own time is a good idea, but not with a timepiece that has a loud ticker. If you use a watch, take it off and place it nearby but not so that it distracts you. And silence your cell phone.

To the best of our ability, we have compiled the content you need to know in this book and in the accompanying online resources. The rest is up to you. You can use the study and testing tips or you can follow your own methods. Either way, you can be confident that there aren't any missing pieces of information and there shouldn't be any surprises in the content on the test.

If you have questions about test fees, registration, electronic testing, or other content verification issues please visit www.mtel.nesinc.com.

Good luck!
Sharon Wynne
Founder, XAMonline

DOMAIN I   ENGLISH LANGUAGE LISTENING PROFICIENCY

COMPETENCY 1.0   THE CANDIDATE WILL APPLY LITERAL LISTENING COMPREHENSION SKILLS IN ENGLISH

Skill 1.1   Identifying stated main ideas, details, sequences, and cause-and effect relationships in a variety of listening situations

In current ESL practice, students are being asked to listen to materials and different speakers and to respond to what they hear. Methods today require an interaction on the part of the listener. This may be a simple nod of the head, answering workbook exercises or performing an action.

To promote autonomy in the learner, Leshinsky (1995) recommends using a listening journal. In this journal, the listener summarizes what he/she listened to three times a week. Each exercise should be 30 minutes long. Suggestions are a TV program, a video, a movie, or a lecture.

In the ESL classroom, English Language Learners (ELLs) usually encounter three types of listening sources (Díaz-Rico, 2008):

- prerecorded selections by various native speakers: simulations of actual conversations
- audiotaped selections from various sources: brief formal lecture, a more informal presentation of same/similar material, and a question and answer section with speakers "from the real world"
- listening to real world sources: university lectures, TV game shows and answering workbook exercises

In each case, the listener develops listening skills through listen practice exercises which gradually increase in difficulty. It is common to encounter non-native speakers in this type of exercise.

Skill 1.2   Identifying steps described in a set of oral directions

When teaching students how to understand efferent (Rosenblatt, 2005) listening ✳(listening to understand messages and to carry away meaning)✳ Tompkins (2009) recommends **four strategies** for maximum effectiveness.

[handwritten notes: ① Organization - patterns ② Summarizing - finding main ideas ③ Getting clues from the speaker ④ Monitoring - active listening vs zoning out]

- **Organization**
  Students need to learn the basic patterns of expository text structures used in informational presentations. These are the same ones found in reading texts: description, comparison, sequence, cause and effect, and problem and solution. In sequence texts, key words such as *first, second, third, next, then, in addition, at last,* and *finally* can be taught so that students recognize the pattern being used.

Teaching students how to identify steps in a set of oral directions is not easy. However, students can be guided through activities which emphasize listening for key points. By preparing advanced organizers, the ELL may concentrate on what is required to complete the activity. Organizers may be prepared in advance and should be closely related to the task to avoid confusion.

- **Summarizing**
  The instructor can ask students to listen for two or three main ideas. These may be written on the board and circled. Students are asked to raise their hands as they hear the main ideas mentioned. Other information can be chunked around the main ideas.

- **Getting clues from the speaker**
  Speakers use many visual and verbal clues to get their message across. Students need to learn to recognize them.
  - **Visual clues**
    Gestures
    Facial expressions
    Writing on the whiteboard
    Underlining information on the whiteboard

  - **Verbal clues**
    Pausing
    Slowing down speech to emphasize key points
    Raising or lowering the voice

- **Monitoring**
  Teaching students to monitor their listening habits is an important strategy because they need to be aware of when they are actively listening or have "zoned out". They can ask the following questions at the beginning of a listening activity:
  - Why am I listening to this message?
  - Will I need to take notes?
  - Does this information make sense to me?

  Later on, during the activity, they may ask the following questions:
  - Is my strategy still working?
  - Am I organizing the information effectively?
  - Is the speaker giving me clues about the organization of the message?
  - Is the speaker giving me nonverbal clues, such as gestures and facial expressions?

It may be necessary for the teacher to guide the students through the process by stopping and helping them with the questions. Monitoring is important in many language arts activities because they need to be aware of the effectiveness of their learning and if it meets their purposes.

Skill 1.3   Choosing an appropriate response to a question or comment based on explicitly stated information

Guiding ELLs through the process of responding to listening activities, both formal and informal, requires patience and creativity. Oftentimes, the lack of oral response in class may be from a cultural difference. Many foreign cultures find it difficult to spontaneously interact as do native speaking Americans. Other possibilities are that the students are embarrassed to admit they do not understand, or simply don't know what to say (Kehe and Kehe 1998 in Díaz-Rico, 2004).

However, since language develops best when practiced, it is necessary to encourage ELLs to practice speaking in informal ways. Pappamihiel (2002 in Díaz-Rico, 2004) suggests that allowing both English and the native language may help reduce anxiety for ELLs as they are developing their language skills. *aka Spanglish / opposite of a English submersion course*

Helping ELLs develop their Basic Interpersonal Communication Skills (BICS) students overcome the challenge knowing what to say and how to say it. Cummins (1984) says that BICS are context embedded as factors other than the linguistic code contribute to meaning. Factors such as voice and gestures can also contribute to meaning.

To teach ELLs how to respond appropriately then, involves giving adequate, guided practice. In addition, non-threatening encouragement is will lower the affective filter allowing the message to be received. When comprehensible input is received, appropriate responses can be obtained.

Skill 1.4   Selecting an accurate paraphrase of an oral message

The classroom atmosphere for ELLs must be a non-threatening, relaxed atmosphere where everyone is encouraged to speak and have their opinions valued. As speaking skills develop, ELLs will develop the ability to paraphrase the oral message.

ELLs need ample opportunities to develop their paraphrasing skills. Some of the activities that are appropriate for developing these skills are: problem solving in small groups, practicing persuasive or entertaining speeches, role plays, interviews, chain stories, talks, problems and discussions (Zelman, 1996 in Díaz-Rico, 2004). Another way would be to have ELLs retell stories they hear in class and change the ending. *

Tompkins (2009) suggests that students can illustrate or paraphrase lines of poems to add to their pictures. This could also be done as an oral activity.

Paraphrasing skills
- Problem solving in sm. groups
- persuasive/entertaining speeches
- role plays
- interviews
etc.

Zwiers (2007) uses paraphrasing as a condensing technique. First paragraphs are placed on the overhead projector and the instructor condenses them into one or two sentences. Then, he uses the following prompts to get students to paraphrase their own work:

- How might you say that with fewer sentences?
- How can we condense what you just said?
- How can we synthesize what you all said?
- Let's try to get that into one sentence. It can have multiple clauses.
- Can you paraphrase that for us?

Key words: Synthesize, summarize, monitoring, paraphrasing skills, condense

COMPETENCY 2.0 **THE CANDIDATE WILL APPLY INFERENTIAL AND CRITICAL LISTENING COMPREHENSION SKILLS IN ENGLISH**

Skill 2.1 **Inferring main ideas, details, comparisons, and cause-and effect relationships not explicitly stated in an oral message**

Many messages in English are explicit, but others require the listener to infer meaning. If ELLs understand English rhetoric, they are better prepared to listen for the main idea, details, and comparisons. A lecture session may be taped and played several times for learners to acquire the necessary understanding of an oral message. Students may pair off and compare their sheets to negotiate meaning.

Bloom's Taxonomy divides the way people learn into three domains. One of these is the cognitive domain which emphasizes intellectual outcomes (Barton, 1997). (The other domains are the affective and the psycho-motor.) Teachers can use scaffolding techniques to guide ELLs in making inferences. Questions such as will guide the learner towards making inferences:

- What inference can you make…?
- What conclusions can you draw…?
- What evidence can you find…?
- What ideas justify …?

Skill 2.2 **Drawing conclusions from information provided in an oral message**

Drawing conclusions from information in an oral message is an authentic listening activity. Many ELLs, nevertheless, will not understand the message with only one exposure. ELLs can then be given the opportunity to tape a message, such as a lecture, and listen several times until comprehension is achieved. When the message is understood, they may be asked for their conclusions. This type of scaffolding should be withdrawn gradually in order to encourage a more realistic listening activity.

Barton (1997) suggests that part of analysis is reaching conclusions based on the message being received. To guide the ELL in drawing conclusions, teachers may ask questions, such as:

- What conclusions can you draw…?
- What is the relationship between…?
- Can you make a distinction between…?
- What is the function of…?
- What ideas justify..?

Skill 2.3   Interpreting a commonly used idiomatic expression

Idioms are the assigning of a new, often figurative, meaning to a group of words whose literal meaning is different. Idioms are informal, often colloquial or slang, and are frequently overused (Curry, 1989). Nevertheless, they form an important part of the English language.

Learning idioms is confusing and difficult for most ELLs. Idioms are numerous and generally taught as they are encountered. Instruction in the nature of idioms should encourage ELLs to move beyond the literal interpretation of words to their figurative meaning. To do this, teachers may encourage the illustration of popular idioms showing both their literal meaning and their figurative meaning. This helps ELLs understand that language is flexible and has been used creatively by others.

Another activity would be for teachers to give the literal meaning of an idiom in an illustrative sentence, followed by a paraphrase of the illustrative sentence. For example: In English class, Ms. Price doesn't like for her students to "clown around". Paraphrase: Ms. Price doesn't like for her students to act silly.

Skill 2.4   Characterizing the tone, mood, or point of view of one or more speakers

It is common for foreign students to assign emotions to speakers based on the tone of voice being used. English is a harsh, guttural language when compared with the softer, more melodic tones of other languages, e.g. Spanish.

A fun way to convey that the English speaker really isn't "angry" would be to have students experiment with speaking English using different emotions. Line drawings illustrating different emotions, such as anger, sadness, joy, confusion, and suspicion, could be passed out. The teacher then models each emotion and has the children to mimic them.

Another exercise is to read a short passage using one of the emotions and have the students identify it. Students can then mimic the teacher as they also read in the same tone of voice.

These exercises, not only demonstrate the emotions, but also teach new vocabulary.

Skill 2.5   Analyzing the social context of a spoken exchange or the relationship between speakers

Basic Interpersonal Communication Skills (BICS), which learners must acquire to function in social situations, are generally less demanding than Cognitive Academic Language Proficiency (CALP), and are generally acquired earlier.

socialting   *classroom*

Language proficiency requires both BICS and CALP. While there are clear distinctions between them, there are underlying similarities that contribute to overall language learning. In addition, students should also recognize Common Underlying Proficiency (CUP). These are skills, ideas, and concepts that learners can transfer from their first language to their English learning. Both similarities and differences between languages can help learners understand and learn aspects of English.

Oral conversations are generally spontaneous, and the participants make up their speech as they interact with each other. They make corrections, revise their words, and try to clear up misunderstandings as they go. At times, oral conversations may seem to be disjointed as the interlocutors bring up new and old topics with their companions.

Vygotsky (1986, 2006) argued that children learn through social interactions and that language is both social and an important facilitator of learning. Through interactions with their classmates and adults children learn things they could not learn on their own (Zebroski, 1994 in Tompkins 2009). Since children can learn from their classmates, teachers often place them in small groups for solving problems that they would be unable to do on their own. Teachers can "scaffold" their charges by model or demonstrate tasks, guide children through the task, ask questions, break complex tasks into smaller steps, and supply pieces of information.

Skill 2.6   Assessing the sufficiency of information in an oral message

Teachers can help ELLs judge a sufficiency of information through active listening exercises where they able to complete graphics while listening. Repeated practice will help the students understand what elements are important and what elements are of minor importance.

One technique for scaffolding the ELLs listening skills would be to have the ELLs follow a lecture or classroom presentation by taking notes to answer a set of predetermined questions. As they follow the presentation, they fill in notes in a variety of ways, such as filling in graphics, charts, balloon diagrams, etc. By seeing a visual representation of the information, they are better able to evaluate their learning and determine what additional information is needed to complete the task and gain a fuller understanding of the material.

When giving oral presentations, ELLs may need help in determining what information is important and what information is of secondary nature. Guided instruction in an outline would be valuable in helping the ELL understand how complete the presentation is.

DOMAIN II   **FOUNDATIONS OF SECOND-LANGUAGE INSTRUCTION**

COMPETENCY 3.0   **UNDERSTAND PROCESSES AND STAGES OF LANGUAGE ACQUISITION AND FACTORS AFFECTING SECOND-LANGUAGE DEVELOPMENT**

Skill 3.1   **Major theories of first-language acquisition and second language acquisition and learning (e.g., Vygotsky, Chomsky, Pinker, Krashen, Cummins)**

Contemporary theories of language acquisition have a solid basis in research on many different language learners in many different cultures. These theories have led to a solid basis upon which to base teaching practice and can guide teachers in their interactions with learners of all types.

Between two and three years of age, most children will be able to use language to influence the people closest to them. Research shows that, in general, boys acquire language more slowly than girls, which means we need to consider carefully how we involve boys in activities designed to promote early language and literacy.

Various theories have tried to explain the language acquisition process.

VYGOTSKY: SOCIAL CONSTRUCTIVISM AND LANGUAGE

relationship btw thought + language

Unlike Chomsky and Piaget, Vygotsky's central focus is the relationship between the development of thought and language. He was interested in the ways different languages affect a person's thinking. He suggests that what Piaget saw as the young child's egocentric speech was actually private speech, the child's way of using words to think about something, which progressed from social speech to thinking in words. Vygotsky views language first as social communication, which gradually promotes both language itself and cognition.

CHOMSKY: THE UNIVERSAL HYPOTHESIS

Chomsky's theory, described as nativism asserts that humans are born with a special biological brain mechanism, called a Language Acquisition Device (LAD). His theory supposes that the ability to learn language is innate, that nature is more important than nurture, and that experience using language is only necessary in order to activate the LAD. Chomsky based his assumptions on work in linguistics. His work shows that children's language development is much more complex than what is proposed by behaviorist theory, which asserts that children learn language merely by being rewarded for imitating. However, Chomsky's theory underestimates the influence that thought (cognition) and language have on each other's development.

 Chomsky = LAD

PINKER: LANGUAGE INSTINCT → *Don't use it, you'll lose it*

Pinker argues that humans are born with an innate capacity for language. He states that language is an instinct as children are able to learn language because the "basic organization of grammar is wired into their brains" through biological evolution. Pinker claims language was created by evolution to solve communication problems among social hunter-gathers. He believes language is universal, but the specific structures in the brain are active during a specific critical period of childhood ✳ after which they are disassembled allowing the brain to use this energy for other purposes. Pinker disagrees with theorists who assert that language and thought are the same. He says that they are separate both in the genes and in the mind from other instincts that comprise the human mind.

KRASHEN: THE MONITOR MODEL

Krashen's Monitor Model consists of 5 main hypotheses.

- **The Acquisition/Learning Hypothesis:** Distinguishes between "acquisition", a subconscious event resulting from natural communication where emphasis is on communication and "learning" which occurs as the result of conscious study of formal properties of language.
- **The Natural Order Hypothesis:** Claims learners follow a more or less invariable path when learning a language and that grammatical structures are acquired in a predictable order.
- **The Monitor Hypothesis:** States a learner uses an internal Monitor to edit "learned" language production. The conditions must include: sufficient time, focus on form and not on meaning, and the user must know the grammar rule.
- **The Input Hypothesis:** Is based on Krashen's belief that "acquisition" takes place when the learner is exposed to comprehensible input a little beyond the learner's current level of competence, or at "I + 1".
- **The Affective Filter Hypothesis:** Controls the amount of input a learner comes in contact with and how much of that input is becomes intake. The Affective Filter is low in learners with high motivation and self-confidence, but high in learners with low motivation and self-confidence. The Affective Filter does not affect the route of language development.

✗ CUMMINS: BICS AND CALPS ✗

Cummins is distinguishes between Basic Interpersonal Communication Skills (BICS) and Cognitive Academic Language Proficiency (CALPS). BICS are the "surface" skills that language students acquire quickly. CALPS are skills needed to perform in an academic setting. Cummins states that children can acquire BICS in approximately 2 years of immersion in the target language, CALPS need between 5-7 years to develop.

PIAGET: COGNITIVE CONSTRUCTIVISM

Piaget's central interest was children's cognitive development. He theorized that language is simply one way that children represent their familiar worlds, a reflection of thought, and that language does not contribute to the development of thinking. He believed that cognitive development precedes language development.

RECENT THEORIZING: INTENTIONALITY

Some contemporary researchers and theorists criticize earlier theories and suggest that children, their behaviors, and their attempts to understand and communicate are misunderstood when the causes of language development are thought to be "outside" the child or mechanistically "in the child's brain." They recognize that children are active learners who co-construct their worlds. Children's language development is part of their holistic development, emerging from cognitive, emotional, and social interactions. These theorists believe that language development depends on the child's social and cultural environment, the people in it, and their interactions. The way children represent these factors in their minds is fundamental to language development. They believe that a child's agenda and the interactions generated by the child promote language learning. The adult's role, actions, and speech are still considered important, but adults need to be able to "mind read" and adjust their side of the co-construction to relate to an individual child's understanding and interpretation.

Theories about language development help us see that enjoying "proto-conversations" with babies (treating them as people who understand, share, and have intentions in sensitive interchanges), and truly listening to young children are the best ways to promote their language development.

Brain research has shown that the single most important factor affecting language acquisition is the onset of puberty. Before puberty, a person uses one area of the brain for language learning; after puberty, a different area of the brain is used. A person who learns a second language before reaching puberty will always process language learning as if prepubescent. A person who begins to learn a second language after the onset of puberty will likely find language learning more difficult and depend more on repetition.

Other researchers have focused on analyzing aspects of the language to be acquired. Factors they consider include:

- **Error analysis:** Recognizing patterns of errors
- **Interlanguage:** Analyzing which aspects of the target language are universal
- **Developmental patterns:** The order in which features of a language are acquired and the sequence in which a specific feature is acquired

Skill 3.2   Characteristics of various stages of first- and second language acquisition

Language acquisition is a gradual, hierarchical, and cumulative process. This means that learners must go through and master each stage in sequence, much as Piaget theorized for learning in general. In terms of syntax, this means learners must acquire specific grammatical structures, first recognizing the difference between subject and predicate; putting subject before predicate; and then learning more complex variations, such as questions, negatives, and relative clauses.

While learners much pass through each stage and accumulate the language skills learned progressively at each stage, learners use different approaches to mastering these skills. Some learners use more cognitive processing procedures; more of their learning takes place through thought processes. Other learners tend to use psycholinguistic procedures, processing learning through more speaking. Regardless of how learners process information, they must all proceed through the same stages, from the least to the most complicated.

Experts disagree on the exact definition of the phases, but a set of six general stages would include:

Stage of Development	Examples
1. Single words	I; throw; ball
2. SVO structure	I throw the ball.
3. Wh-fronting	Where you are?
Do fronting	Do you like me?
Adverb fronting	Today I go to school.
Negative + verb	She is not nice.
4. Y/N inversion	Do you know him? Yes, I know him.
Copula (linking v) inversion	Is he at school?
Particle shift	Take your hat off.
5. Do 2nd	Why did she leave?
Aux 2nd	Where has he gone?
Neg do 2nd	She does not live here.
6. Cancel inversion	I asked what she was doing.

Each progressive step requires the learner to use knowledge from the previous step, as well as new knowledge of the language. As ELLs progress to more advanced stages of syntax, they may react differently, depending on their ability to acquire the new knowledge that is required for mastery

Skill 3.3   **Cognitive processes involved in internalizing language rules and learning vocabulary in a second language (e.g., memorization, categorization, metacognition)**

COGNITIVE STRATEGIES = PRAC

Cognitive strategies are vital to second-language acquisition; their most salient feature is the manipulation of the second language. The most basic strategies are: practicing, receiving and sending messages, analyzing and reasoning, and creating structure for input and output, which can be remembered by the acronym PRAC.

- **Practicing:** Practice constant repetition, make attempts to imitate a native speaker's accent, concentrate on sounds, and practice in a realistic setting to help promote the learner's grasp of the language.
- **Receiving and sending messages:** These strategies help the learner quickly locate salient points and then interpret the meaning: skim through information to determine "need to know" vs. "nice to know," use available resources (print and non-print) to interpret messages.
- **Analyzing and reasoning:** Use general rules to understand the meaning and then work into specifics, and break down unfamiliar expressions into parts.
- **Creating structure for input and output:** Choose a format for taking meaningful notes; practice summarizing long passages; use highlighters as a way to focus on main ideas or important specific details.

METACOGNITIVE STRATEGIES

The ESOL teacher is responsible for helping students become aware of their own individual learning strategies and constantly improve and add to those strategies. Each student should have his/her own toolbox of skills for planning, managing, and evaluating the language-learning process.

Some salient points for ELLs to keep in mind:

- **Center your learning:** Review a key concept or principle and link it to existing knowledge, make a firm decision to pay attention to the general concept, ignore input that is distracting, and learn skills in the proper order.
- **Arrange and plan your learning:** Take the time to understand how a language is learned; create optimal learning conditions, i.e., regulate noise, lighting, and temperature; obtain the appropriate books, etc.; and set reasonable long- and short-term goals.
- **Evaluate your learning:** Keep track of errors that prevent further progress and keep track of progress, e.g., reading faster now than the previous month.

SOCIOAFFECTIVE STRATEGIES

Socioaffective strategies are broken down into affective and social strategies. **Affective strategies** are those that help the learner control the emotions and attitudes that hinder progress in learning the second language and at the same time help him/her learn to interact in a social environment. There are three sets of affective strategies—lowering your anxiety, encouraging yourself, and taking your emotional temperature—which are easy to remember with the acronym LET.

[handwritten note in left margin: LET (3 sets of affective strategies)]

- **Lowering your anxiety:** These strategies try to maintain emotional equilibrium with physical activities: Use meditation and/or deep breathing to relax, listen to calming music, and read a funny book or watch a comedy.
- **Encouraging yourself:** These strategies help support and motivate the learner. Stay positive through self-affirmations, take risks, and give yourself rewards.

- **Taking your emotional temperature:** These strategies help learners control their emotions by understanding what they are feeling emotionally as well as why they are feeling that way. Listen to your body's signals; create a checklist to keep track of feelings and motivations during the second-language-acquisition process; keep a diary to record progress and feelings; and share feelings with a classmate or friend.

Social strategies affect how the learner interacts in a social setting. The following are three useful strategies for interacting socially: asking questions, cooperating with others, and empathizing with others, which can be remembered with the acronym ACE.

- **Asking questions:** Ask for clarification or help. Request that the speaker slow down, repeat, or paraphrase, and ask to be corrected when you are speaking.
- **Cooperating with others:** Interact with more than one person: Work cooperatively with a partner or small group and work with a native speaker of the language.
- **Empathizing with others:** Learn how to relate to others, remembering that people usually have more things in common than things that set them apart. Empathize with another student by learning about his/her culture and being aware and sensitive to his/her thoughts and feelings. Understanding and empathizing will help the other student but it will also help the empathizer.

PRIOR KNOWLEDGE

Schemata, or the prior knowledge students have when beginning a new foreign language, is a valuable asset to be exploited in their language learning. The schema theory (Carrell and Eisterhold, 1983) explains how the brain processes knowledge and how this facilitates comprehension and learning. A schema is the framework around information that is stored in the brain. As new information is received, schemata are activated to store the new information. By connecting what is known with what is being learned, understanding is achieved and learning can take place. If students lack sufficient prior knowledge, they cannot be expected to understand a new lesson.

Children may or may not have prior educational experiences upon which to build their new language skills. However, even children who have little or no formal education may have been taught the alphabet or simple mathematics by their parents. Children from oral cultures may have quite sophisticated language structures already in place upon which to base new language learning.

COGNITIVE/LEARNING STYLES

A student's learning style includes cognitive, affective, and psychological behaviors that indicate his/her characteristic and consistent way of perceiving, interacting with, and responding to the learning environment (Willing, 1988).

Willing identified four main learning styles used by ESL learners in Australia:

Know the Difference!

- **Concrete learning style:** People-oriented, emotional, and spontaneous
- **Analytic learning style:** Object-oriented, with the capacity for making connections and inferences
- **Communicative learning style:** Autonomous, prefers social learning, likes making decisions
- **Authority-oriented learning style:** Defers to the teacher, does not enjoy learning by discovery, intolerant of facts that do not fit (ambiguity)

Reid (1987) identified four perceptual learning tendencies:

- **Visual learning:** Learning mainly from seeing words in books, on the board, etc.
- **Auditory learning:** Learning by hearing words spoken and from oral explanations, from listening to tapes or lectures
- **Kinesthetic learning:** Learning by experience, by being involved physically in classroom experiences
- **Tactile learning:** Hands-on learning, learning by doing, working on models, lab experiments, etc.

Skill 3.4   **Factors affecting second-language acquisition (e.g., age, motivation, learning style, environmental factors) and the role of the first language in second-language development (e.g., language transfer, interlanguage development)**

While there is a continuous effort to establish a "Standard English" to be taught for English Language Learners (ELLs), English learning and acquisition depends on the **cultural and linguistic background** of the ELL, as well as preconceived perceptions of English Language cultural influences. These factors can act as a filter, causing confusion and inhibiting learning. Since language by definition is an attempt to share knowledge, the cultural, ethnic, and linguistic diversity of learners influences both their own history as well as how they approach and learn a new language.

Teachers must assess the ELL to determine how cultural, ethnic, and linguistic experience can impact the student's learning. This evaluation should take into account many factors, including:

- The cultural background and educational sophistication of the ELL
- The exposure of the ELL to various English language variants and cultural beliefs

No single approach, program, or set of practices fits all students' needs, backgrounds, and experiences. The ideal program for a Native American teenager attending an isolated tribal school may fail to reach a Hispanic youth enrolled in an inner city or suburban district.

CULTURAL FACTORS

Culture encompasses the sum of human activity and symbolic structures that have significance and importance for a particular group of people. Culture is manifested in language, customs, history, arts, beliefs, institutions and other representative characteristics, and is a means of understanding the lives and actions of people.

Customs play an important part in language learning because they directly affect interpersonal exchanges. What is polite in one culture might be offensive in another. For example, in the U. S., making direct eye contact is considered polite and not to make eye contact connotes deviousness, inattention, or rude behavior. The custom in many Asian cultures is exactly the opposite. Teachers who are unaware of this cultural difference can easily offend an Asian ELL and unwittingly cause a barrier to learning. However, teachers who are familiar with this custom can make efforts not to offend the learner and can teach the difference between the two customs so that the ELL can learn how to interact without allowing contrary customs to interfere.

Beliefs and institutions have a strong emotional influence on ELLs and should always be respected. While customs should be adaptable, similar to switching registers when speaking, no effort should be made to change the beliefs or institutional values of an ELL. Presenting new ideas is a part of growth, learning, and understanding. Even though the beliefs and values of different cultures often have irreconcilable differences, they should be addressed. In these instances teachers must respect alternative attitudes and adopt an "agree to disagree" attitude. Presenting new, contrasting points of view should not be avoided because new ideas can strengthen original thinking as well as change it. All presentations should be neutral, however, and no effort should be made to alter a learner's thinking. While addressing individual cultural differences, teachers should also teach tolerance of all cultures. This attitude is especially important in a culturally diverse classroom, but will serve all students well in their future interactions.

Studying the **history and various art forms** of a culture reveals much about the culture and offers opportunities to tap into the interests and talents of ELLs. Comparing the history and art of different cultures encourages critical thinking and often reveals commonalities as well as differences, leading to greater understanding among people.

Culture constitutes a rich component of language learning. It offers a means of drawing learners into the learning process and greatly expands their understanding of a new culture, as well as their own. Second language acquisition, according to the findings of Saville-Troike (1986), places the learner in the position of having to learn a second culture. The outcome of learning a second culture can have negative or positive results, not only depending on how teaching is approached, but also outside factors. How people in the new culture respond to ELLs makes them feel welcome or rejected. The attitudes and behavior of the learner's family are particularly important. If the family is supportive and embraces the second culture, then the effect is typically positive. However, if acculturation is perceived as rejecting the primary culture, then the child risks feeling alienated from both cultures.

Very Interesting

There are many different ways that students are affected by the **cultural differences** in their native culture and home when compared with the culture being acquired through schooling and daily life in a foreign culture.

The following points, adapted from Peregoy and Boyle (2008), illustrate some of the many different ways that culture affects us daily and thus affect students in their participation, learning, and adjustment to a different society and its schools.

- **Family structures:** What constitutes a family? What are the rights and responsibilities of each family member? What is the hierarchy of authority?
- **Life cycles:** What are the criteria for defining stages, periods or transitions in life? What rites of passage are there? What behaviors are considered appropriate for children of different ages? How might these conflict with behaviors taught or encouraged in school?
- **Roles and interpersonal relationships:** How do the roles of girls and women differ from those of boys and men? How do people greet each other? Do girls work and interact with boys? Is deference shown, and to whom and by whom?
- **Discipline:** What is discipline? Which behaviors are considered socially acceptable for boys versus girls at different ages? Who or what is considered responsible if a child misbehaves? The child? Parents? Older siblings? The environment? Is blame even ascribed? Who has authority over whom? How is behavior traditionally controlled? To what extent and in what domains?
- **Time and space:** How important is punctuality? How important is speed in completing a task? How much space are people accustomed to? What significance is associated with different cultural locations or directions, including north, south, east, and west?
- **Religion:** What restrictions are there on topics discussed in school? Are dietary restrictions to be observed, including fasting? What restrictions are associated with death and the dead?
- **Food:** What is eaten? In what order and how often is food eaten? Which foods are restricted? Which foods are typical? What social obligations are there with regard to food giving, reciprocity, and honoring people? What restrictions or proscriptions are associated with handling, offering, or discarding food?
- **Health and hygiene:** How are illnesses treated and by whom? What is to be considered the cause? If a student were involved in an accident at school, would any of the common first aid practices be unacceptable?
- **History, traditions, and holidays:** Which events and people are sources of pride for this group? To what extent does the group in the United States identify with the history and traditions of the country of origin? What holidays and celebrations are considered appropriate for observing in school? Which ones are appropriate for private observance?
- **Age:** Can impact second language acquisition, as well, when a culture determines what a person does, as well as when they can do it. For example,

as noted by Sindell (1988), middle-class European Americans tend to expect that children will play and behave appropriately for their age, rather than take on more adult responsibilities. In contrast, young Cree Indian children are expected to carry out many adult responsibilities. Furthermore, many Cree Indian parents disapprove of academic activities because they distract the children from involvement in the Cree Indian society.

AGE

Not only is age important in the role of the ELL in his society, but age is important in the maturing processes which affect language learning. According to Ellis (1985), age does not affect the "route" (order) of second-language acquisition (SLA). Thus, children and adults acquire language in the same order, that is, they go through the same stages. With respect to rate of acquisition, teens appear to surpass both children and adults, especially in learning the grammatical system (Snow and Hoefnagel-Hohle, 1978). Older learners seem to be more efficient learners. The achievement of a foreign language is strongly related to the amount of time spent on the language, and the earlier a second language is started, the better the pronunciation (Burstall et al., 1974). Krashen (1982) disagrees, believing instead that SLA is related to the amount of comprehensible input (i.e., the younger child will receive more comprehensible input) and that younger learners are more open emotionally to SLA.

Other theorists have formulated different hypotheses about age in SLA related to affective factors. In the critical period hypothesis, Penfield and Roberts (1959) state that the first ten years are the best age for SLA as the brain retains its plasticity. After puberty, this plasticity disappears and the flexibility required for SLA is lost. Guiora et al. (1972) believe that around the age of puberty, the ability to acquire native-like pronunciation of the foreign language is no longer present.

Cognitive explanations are also used to explain the effects of age on SLA. These theories assert that children are more prone to use their Language Acquisition Device (LAD), while adults are better able to use their inductive reasoning because of more fully developed cognitive faculties. Rosansky (1975) explains SLA in terms of Piaget's "period of concrete operations." Rosansky believes the child is more open and flexible to new language than an adult who identifies more closely with the differences in the native language and the language to be acquired. Krashen (1982) believes that adolescents and adults probably have greater access to comprehensible input than children and that this is the real causative variable, rather than age itself.

AFFECTIVE FACTORS

The term **affective domain** refers to the feelings and emotions in human behavior that affect how a second language is acquired. Self-esteem, motivation, anxiety, and attitude all contribute to the second language acquisition process. Internal and external factors influence the affective domain. ESOL teachers must be aware of each student's personality and must stay especially attuned to the affective factors in their students.

- **Self-esteem:** Learning a second language puts learners in a vulnerable frame of mind. While some learners are less inhibited about taking risks, all learners can easily be shut down if their comfort level is surpassed. Using teaching techniques that lower stress and emphasize group participation, rather than focusing on individuals getting the right answer, reduces anxiety and encourages learners to attempt to use the new language.
- **Motivation:** Researchers Gardner and Lambert (1972) have identified two types of motivation in relation to learning a second language:
  - **Instrumental motivation:** Acquiring a second language for a specific reason, such as a job
  - **Integrative motivation:** Acquiring a second language to fulfill a wish to communicate within a different culture

  Neither type stands completely alone. Instructors recognize that motivation can be viewed as either a "trait" or a "state." As a trait motivation is more permanent and culturally acquired, whereas as a state, motivation is considered temporary because it fluctuates, depending on rewards and penalties.

- **Anxiety:** Anxiety is inherent in second-language learning. Students are required to take risks, such as speaking in front of their peers. Without a native's grasp of the language, second language learners are unable to express their individuality, which is even more threatening and uncomfortable. However, not all anxiety is debilitative. Bailey's (1983) research on "facilitative anxiety" (anxiety that compels an individual to stay on task) is a positive factor for some learners, closely related to competitiveness.
- **Attitudes:** Attitude typically evolves from internalized feelings about oneself and one's ability to learn a language. On the other hand, one's attitude about language and the speakers of that language is largely external and is influenced by the surrounding environment of classmates and family.

If non-native speakers of English experience discrimination because of their accent or cultural status, their attitude toward the value of Second Language Learning may diminish. Schools can significantly improve the attitude towards SLAs by encouraging activities between native speakers and ELLs. This can be particularly beneficial to both groups if students learning the SLA's first language work on projects together. When native speakers get a chance to appreciate the SLA's language skill in their first language, attitudes change and ELLs have an opportunity to shine.

In some cultures, children who learn a second language at the expense of their primary language might be viewed as "turncoats" by family and friends.

This can cause negative feelings about school in general and can adversely affect second language acquisition.

LEARNING STYLES

Students have different learning styles that affect the way in which they learn and are able to express themselves. Oftentimes, there are cultural factors which affect their learning styles (e.g. role of minors in the family structure and their society, the learning/teaching styles used in the native culture, the ability to "look the speaker in the eye", and the distance between speakers). Individual learning styles within cultures affect ELLs differently.

Researchers have devoted considerable time to analyzing learning styles. Learning styles may fit into more than one category, and students may exhibit more than one type of learning style.

RESEARCHERS	LEARNING STYLES
Hruska-Reichmann and Grasha (1982)	• Competitive vs. cooperative • Dependent vs. independent • Participant vs. avoidant
Keefe (1987)	• Physiological variables (nutrition, health, time of day preferences, sleeping and waking habits, need for mobility, and needs for and response to varying levels of light, sound, and temperature) • Affective variables (amount of structure of supervision student needs, level of anxiety or curiosity student displays, degree of persistence in face of frustration) • Incentive variables (personal interests, level of achievement motivation, enjoyment of competition vs. cooperation, risk taking vs. caution, reaction to rewards vs. punishment, social motivation coming from family, school, and ethnic background, and internal vs. external control) • Cognitive variables (field dependent vs. field independent, conceptual/analytical vs. perceptual/concrete, broad vs. focused attention, easily distracted vs. capable of controlled concentration, leveling {tendency to lump new experiences with previous ones} vs. sharpening {ability to distinguish small differences}, high cognitive complexity {accepting of diverse, perhaps conflicting input} vs. low cognitive complexity {tendency to reduce conflicting information to a minimum})
Sonbucher (1991)	• Combination of information-processing styles (preferences for reading, writing, listening, speaking, visualizing, or manipulating) and work environment

	preferences (such as differences in motivation, concentration, length of study sessions, involvement with others, level of organization, prime times for study, amount of noise, light, heat and need for food/drink
Tharp (1989)	• Identified two sets of contrasting learning styles: visual/verbal and holistic/analytic. Schools typically prefer students who are verbal and analytical.
Kolb (1976)	• Studied adult learners and developed a theory of experiential learning. Four-stage process: a learner's experience forms the basis for observation and reflection, which in turn permits the learner to make decisions and solve problems, creating the basis for new experiences. • Four learning types: active experimentation vs. reflective observation and abstract conceptualization vs. concrete experience
McCarthy (1983)	Four learning styles similar to Kolb's learning styles • Innovative: personally involved through social interaction • Analytic learner: thinks through ideas and concepts • Commonsense learner: hands-on experience and enjoys solving practical problems • Dynamic learner: uses intuition and trial and error, taking risks and jumping to conclusions
Gregorc (1982)	Explored the differences in teaching styles and learning styles. Categorized learners into 4 types: • Abstract random • Abstract sequential • Concrete random • Concrete sequential
Myers/Briggs (See Murphy, J.M., 1998 and Keirsey, D. 1998).	Based on Jung's theory of personality Classified learners into 4 opposing dimensions which when combined make up 16 different dimensions • Introversion/extroversion • Sensing/perception • Thinking/feeling • Judging/perceiving

Adapted from Díaz-Rico, 2008.

EDUCATIONAL EXPERIENCE

ELLs come to the United States for many different reasons: in search of a better life, fleeing war zones and oppressive governments, or to escape economic difficulties. In many cases, ELLs have entered the school system in their native land and done very well. In other cases, they have had little or no educational experience. In either case, it is imperative that, previous to or upon enrollment, assessment of the student take place—if possible, in their L1. By building on their previous knowledge with regard to literacy, language, and experience, L2 instruction will be more successful (Au, 1993, 2002; Ovando et al., 2006).

Shumm (2006) emphasizes that not only are reading-level characteristics important, but also the differences between L1 and L2, as these may influence the assumed level of the student. Some of the questions she proposes for eliciting these similarities and differences are useful for further evaluation of reading-level characteristics:

- Is the L1 writing system logographic, as is Arabic; syllabic, as is Cherokee; or alphabetic, as are English and Greek?
- How does the L1 syntax compare with L2 syntax?
- Are the spelling patterns phonetic with consistent grapheme-phoneme relationships (e.g., Spanish or French), or are there multiple vowel sounds (e.g., English)?
- Do students read from left to right and top to bottom in their L1?
- Are there true cognates (Spanish: *instrucción*, and English: *instruction*) and false cognates (Spanish: *librería* [bookstore], and English: *library*) that will help or confuse the ELL?
- Are the discourse patterns and writing styles of L1 and L2 similar or different?
- Are questions with known answers asked (teacher questions) or are rhetorical questions (found among many working-class families) asked?
- Is L1 writing style circular, with long sentences and many details (e.g., Spanish), or linear, with the minimum number of facts or supporting details needed to support the main idea (e.g., English)?

POSITIVE AND NEGATIVE LANGUAGE TRANSFER
L1 transfer refers to the effect the native tongue has on the language being acquired. It can be positive or negative. **Negative transfer** is illustrated in many of the errors ELLs make when using the new language. An example would be Chinese learners who overuse expressions of regret when apologizing because in their native language it is customary to do so.

Positive transfer occurs when similar structures in the L1 facilitate the learning of the new language. An example of this would be when cognates are able to transfer to the target language.

INTERLANGUAGE DEVELOPMENT
Interlanguage is a strategy used by a second language learner to compensate for his/her lack of proficiency while learning a second language. It cannot be classified as first language (L1), nor can it be classified as a second language (L2), rather it could almost be considered a third language (L3), complete with its own grammar and lexicon. Interlanguage is developed by the learner, in relation to the learner's experiences (both positive and negative) with the second language. Larry Selinker introduced the theory of interlanguage in 1972 and asserted that L2 learners create

certain learning strategies, to "compensate" in this in-between period, while the learner acquires the language.

Interlanguage Learning Strategies	
Overgeneralization	Overgeneralization occurs when the learner attempts to apply a rule "across-the-board," without regard to irregular exceptions. For example, a learner is over-generalizing when he/she attempts to apply an "ed" to create a past tense for an irregular verb, such as "buyed" or "swimmed."
Simplification	Simplification refers to the L2 learner using resources that require limited vocabulary to aid comprehension and allow the learner to listen, read, and speak in the target language at a very elementary level.
L1 interference or language transfer	L1 Interference or language transfer occurs when a learner's primary language influences his/her progress in the secondary language, L2. Interference most commonly affects pronunciation, grammar structures, vocabulary and semantics

Selinker theorizes that a psychological structure is "awakened" when a learner begins the process of second language acquisition. He attached great significance to the notion that the learner and the native speaker would not create similar sounds if they attempted to communicate the same thought, idea, or meaning.

Fossilization is a term applied by Selinker to the process in which an L1 leaner reaches a plateau and accepts that less-than fluent level, which prevents the learner from achieving L2 fluency. Fossilization occurs when non-L1 forms become fixed in the interlanguage of the L2 learner. L2 learners are highly susceptible to this phenomenon during the early stages.

COMPETENCY 4.0	UNDERSTAND THE BASIC LINGUISTIC AND SOCIOLINGUISTIC CONCEPTS RELATED TO INSTRUCTION FOR ENGLISH LEARNERS

Skill 4.1   Knowledge of phonetics and phonemics (e.g., distinguishing among classes of sound)

The definition of **phonology** can be summarized as "the way in which speech sounds form patterns" (Diaz-Rico, Weed, 1995). Phonology is a subset of the linguistics field, which studies the organization and systems of sound within a particular language. Phonology is based on the theory that every native speaker unconsciously retains the sound structure of his or her language and is more concerned with the sounds than with the physical process of creating those sounds.

When babies babble or make what we call baby sounds, they are actually experimenting with all of the sounds represented in all languages. As they learn a specific language, they become more proficient in the sounds of that language and forget how to make sounds that they don't need or use.

Phonemes, pitch, and **stress** are all components of phonology. Because each affects the meaning being communicated, they are variables that ELLs must recognize and learn.

Phonology analyzes the sound structure of the given language by:

- determining which phonetic sounds have the most significance
- explaining how these sounds influence a native speaker of the language

For example, the Russian alphabet has a consonant, which, when pronounced, sounds like the French word, "*rouge*". English speakers typically have difficulty pronouncing this sound pattern, because inherently they know this is not a typical English-language sound--although it is encountered occasionally (Díaz-Rico, Weed, 1995).

Mastering a sound that does not occur in the learner's first language requires ongoing repetition, both of hearing the sound and attempting to say it. The older the learner, the more difficult this process becomes, especially if the learner has spoken only one language before reaching puberty. Correct pronunciation may literally require years of practice because initially the learner may not hear the sound correctly. Expecting an ELL to master an English pronunciation quickly leads to frustration for the teacher and the learner. With enough focused repetition, however, the learner may eventually hear the difference and be able to imitate it. Inadequate listening and speaking practice will result in a persistent heavy accent.

A Phoneme is the smallest unit of sound that affects meaning, i.e., distinguishes one word from another. In English, there are approximately 44 speech sounds yet only 26 letters, so the sounds, when combined, become words. For this reason, English is not considered a phonetic language—a language of one-to-one correspondence between letters and sounds. For example, consider the two words, "pin" and "bin." The only difference is the first consonant of the words, the "p" in "pin" and "b" in "bin." The sounds "p" and "b" are phonemes in spoken English, because the difference in sound creates a difference in meaning.

Focusing on phonemes to provide pronunciation practice allows students to have fun while they learn to recognize and say sounds Pairs or groups of words that have a set pattern make learning easier For example, students can practice saying words that rhyme but begin with a different phoneme, such as tan, man, fan, and ran Other groups of words might start with the same phoneme followed by various vowel sounds, such as ten, ton, tan, and tin This kind of alliteration can be used to compose tongue twisters that students find challenging and fun

Vowels and consonants should be introduced in a deliberate order to allow combinations that form real words, though made up words that have no real meaning in English should also be encouraged when introducing new sounds

Pitch in communication determines the context or meaning of words or series of words A string of words can communicate more than one meaning when posed as a question or statement For example, the phrase "I can't go" acts as a statement, if the pitch or intonation falls However, the same phrase becomes the question "I can't go?" if the pitch or intonation rises for the word "go"

Stress can occur at a "word" or "sentence" level. At the "word" level, different stresses on the syllable can actually modify the word's meaning. Consider the word "conflict." To pronounce it as a noun, one would stress the first syllable, as in "*CON*flict." However, when used as a verb, the second syllable would be stressed, as in "con*FLICT*." Different dialects sometimes pronounce the same word differently, even though both pronunciations have the same meaning. For example, in some parts of the United States the word "insurance" is pronounced by stressing the second syllable, while in other parts of the country the first syllable is stressed.

At the "sentence" level, stress can also be used to vary the meaning. For example, consider the following questions and how the meaning changes, according to the stressed words:

> **He** did that? (Emphasis is on the person.)
> He **did** that? (Emphasis is on the action.)
> He did **that**? (Emphasis is on object of the action.)

This type of meaning differentiation is difficult for most ELL students to grasp, and requires innovative teaching methods, such as acting out the three different meanings. However, since pitch and stress can change the meaning of a sentence completely, students must learn to recognize these differences. Not recognizing sarcasm or anger can cause students considerable problems in their academic endeavors and daily interactions.

Phonographemics refers to the study of letters and letter combinations. Unlike Spanish and French and many other languages, in English one symbol can represent many phonemes, and there are multiple pronunciations of vowels and consonants. Phonetic rules are critical to learning to read and write, however, because of the numerous exceptions, the rules themselves do little to assist listening and speaking skills, which makes English a difficult language to learn.

When teaching English to speakers of other languages, the wide variation of phonemes represented by a single symbol must be taught and *drilled*. If it is difficult for native speakers to learn the English spelling system, it is a great leap for the foreign-language learner. Graphemes, the written letter or group of letters that represents a single sound, should be introduced long after spoken English Students must first be able to speak and hear the language before they can be taught to spell it. The phonology of spoken English is an important component of an ESOL program.

Phonographemic differences between English words are a common source of confusion and thus need to be taught explicitly with numerous learning activities in order to enable learners to understand sufficiently the various distinctions. Some areas of focus for the ESOL classroom include:

- **Homonyms:** A general term that describes words that have two or more meanings
- **Homographs:** Two or more words that have the same spelling or pronunciation but different meanings, e.g., stalk (part of a plant) / stalk (follow)
- **Homophones:** Two or more words that have the same pronunciation but different meanings and spellings, e.g., wood/would, cite/sight
- **Heteronyms:** Two or more words that have the same spelling, but have a different pronunciation and meaning, e.g., Polish/polish

Some useful activities for instruction would be to identify misspelled words, to recognize multiple meanings of words in sentences, to spell words correctly within a given context, and to match words with their meanings.

Sound-symbol correspondence is more difficult in English than some other languages because each letter can make a variety of sounds. Recognition of repeating patterns helps students develop decoding skills. Consonant blends such as /ch/, /ph/, and /sh/ are readily recognizable and make the same sound with consistency. Earliest beginners can scan for those language patterns and recognize the sounds they make.

Skill 4.2   Use of morphology and lexicon to analyze a word's structure, function, and meaning

Morphology refers to the process of how the words of a language are formed to create meaningful messages. ESOL teachers need to be aware of the principles of morphology in English in order to provide meaningful activities that will help in the process of language learning.

Morphemic analysis requires breaking a word down into its component parts to determine its meaning. It shows the relationship between the root or base word and the prefix and/or suffix to determine the word's meaning.

A morpheme is the smallest unit of a language system that has meaning these units are more commonly known as: the root word, the prefix, and the suffix, and they cannot be broken down into any smaller units.

- **The root word or base word** is the key to understanding a word, because this is where the actual meaning is determined.
- **A prefix** is a syllable or syllables which appear in front of the root or base word and can alter the meaning of the root or base word.
- **A suffix** is a letter or letters which are added to the end of the word and can alter the original tense or meaning of the root or base word.

The following is an example of how morphemic analysis can be applied to a word:

- Choose a root or base word, such as "kind."
- Create as many new words as possible, by changing the prefix and suffix.
- New words would include "unkind", "kindness", and "kindly."

Learning common roots, prefixes, and suffixes greatly helps ELLs to decode unfamiliar words. This can make a big difference in how well a student understands written language. Students who can decode unfamiliar words become less frustrated when reading in English and, as a result, are likely to enjoy reading more. They have greater comprehension and their language skills improve more quickly. Having the tools to decode unfamiliar words enables ELL students to perform better on standardized tests because they are more likely to understand the question and answer choices.

Guessing at the meaning of words should be encouraged. Too often, students become dependent on translation dictionaries, which can cause students to fail to develop morphemic-analysis skills. Practice should include identifying roots, prefixes, and suffixes, as well as using morphemic knowledge to form new words.

ESOL learners need to understand the structure of words in English, and how words may be created and altered. Some underlying principles of the morphology of English are:

1. Morphemes may be free and able to stand by themselves (e.g., chair, bag), or they may be bound or derivational, needing to be used with other morphemes to create meaning (e.g., read-able, en-able).

2. Knowledge of the meanings of derivational morphemes such as prefixes and suffixes enables students to decode word meanings and create words in the language through word analysis (e.g., un-happy means not happy).

3. Some morphemes in English provide grammatical rather than semantic information to words and sentences (e.g., of, the, and).

4. Words can be combined in English to create new compound words (e.g., key + chain = keychain).

ESOL teachers also need to be aware that principles of morphology from the native language may be transferred to either promote or interfere with the second-language learning process.

When students over generalize a learned rule or simply make a mistake, corrections should be made in a way that does not embarrass the student. Teachers must also consider a student's stage of progress and the context of the error. Correcting every single error is unnecessary when students are experimenting with language and bravely trying to use a language they are struggling to learn. A useful technique is to repeat segments of spoken language, as if to confirm understanding, and correct any errors. This saves face for the student and allows the teacher to demonstrate the correct word use or pronunciation. If the student fails to notice the correction and makes the same error again, the teacher can repeat the same type of correction. Teachers can also demonstrate variations of words in this manner, such as using a different verb tense to paraphrase what was said.

Correcting every error in a writing sample can discourage participation and cause students to shut down to learning. Keeping track of errors that students repeat allows the teacher to reteach specific skills or address specific needs, either with a group of students who all need to master that skill, or individually for a student who has not yet mastered a skill with others in the class.

Recognition of cognates and false cognates is very helpful in decoding and can be directly taught. Many words are identical in English and Spanish, with the only difference being pronunciation. Fortunately for students, as they develop skills in content areas such as math and science, the incidence of these cognates increases. Some examples of English-Spanish cognates are:

- *hotel*
- *radio*
- *religion*
- *eclipse*
- *editor*

Many words are the same in English and Spanish, with the addition of a changed vowel at the end of the word. Here are some examples:

- *cost: costo*
- *cause: causa*
- *minute: minute*
- *medicine: medicina*
- *list: lista*
- *map: mapa*

Here are some of the common false cognates between English and Spanish:

- *libreria*—It's not a *library*, but a *bookstore*
- *embarazada*—It doesn't mean *embarrassed*, but *pregnant*
- *asistir*—It doesn't mean *to help*, but *to attend* or *be present*

Prefixes and suffixes can be directly taught to give the student scaffolding in decoding new words. For instance, *-ful* and *-less* can be taught and then combined with known words to make new ones.

- *Help + ful = helpful*
- *Help + less = helpless*
- *Care + ful = careful*
- *Care + less = careless*

Skill 4.3 Recognition of syntactic features (e.g., a verb phrase) and discourse features in oral and written text (e.g., cohesion)

Syntax involves the order in which words are arranged to create meaning. Different languages use different patterns for sentence structure. Syntax also refers to the rules for creating correct sentence patterns. English, like many other languages, is a subject-verb-object language, i.e., in most sentences the subject precedes the verb, and the object follows the verb. ELLs whose native language follows a subject-verb-object pattern will find it easier to master English syntax.

THE ENGLISH SYNTACTIC SYSTEM

English classifies eight parts of speech, each with a specific role in sentences. Understanding the parts of speech can be quite difficult for ELLs because the same word can have a different role in different sentences, and a different meaning entirely. Identifying the subject and predicate of the sentence helps to distinguish what role a particular word plays in a sentence. Since English is a subject-verb-object (S-V-O) language, the placement of a word in a sentence relative to the subject or verb indicates what part of speech it is.

- That TV *show* was boring.

- I will *show* you my new dress.
- The band plays *show* tunes at half time.

In these examples, the word *show* is first a noun, then a verb, and finally an adjective.

The Eight Parts of Speech	
Noun	A person, place, thing or idea. Common nouns are non-specific, while proper nouns name a particular person, place, thing, or idea, and are capitalized. Nouns may be **countable** or **uncountable**. Countable nouns describe countable objects, e.g., an apple, twelve chairs, six geese, a cup of coffee. Uncountable nouns describe things that cannot be counted, e.g., liberty, coffee, or politics. *Many* and *few* are used when referring to countable nouns, and *much* and *little* when referring to uncountable nouns.
Verb	An action or state of being.

Pronoun	A word that takes the place of a noun. A pronoun refers back to the word it replaces—its **antecedent**.
	There are three types of pronouns:
	• *Personal pronouns* can be
	    ○ first, second, or third person (I, you, he, she, it)
	    ○ singular or plural (I/we, you/you, he, she, it/they)
	    ○ subjective or objective (I/me, you/you, he/him, she/her, it/it, we/us, they/them)
	• *Possessive pronouns* show ownership (my, mine, your, yours, his, her, hers, its, our, ours, your, yours, their, and theirs).
	• *Indefinite pronouns* refer to persons, places, things or ideas in general, such as any, each, both, most, something.

Adjective	A word that modifies a noun or pronoun. Adjectives answer the questions, *What kind? How many?* and *Which?*
Adverb	A word that modifies a verb, an adjective, or another adverb. Adverbs answer the questions, *How? When? Where? How often?* and *To what extent?*
Preposition	A word that, in a phrase with a noun or pronoun, shows the relationship between a noun or pronoun and another word in a sentence. Prepositions describe or show location, direction, or time. Prepositional phrases can have as few as two words, but can include any number of adjectives.
Interjection	A word that shows surprise or strong feeling. An interjection can stand alone (*Help!*) or be used within a sentence (*Oh no, I forgot my wallet!*)

Conjunction	Conjunctions may be either coordinating or subordinating. **Coordinating conjunctions** (*and, but, or, nor*) connect words or phrases that have the same grammatical function in a sentence. The coordinating conjunction pair *either/or* is used for affirmative statements; the pair *neither/nor* is used for negative statements. *Parallel structure* is desired when using coordinating conjunctions, e.g., *to ride, to sing, and to dance.* (Similar structures for clauses are indicated.) The coordinating conjunctions (*so, for, yet*) may also be used to connect two independent clauses. **Subordinating conjunctions** are words used to introduce adverbial clauses. Some* of the subordinating conjunctions used for _____ are:<ul><li>**time**: *after, before, when, while, as, as soon as, since, until*</li><li>**cause and effect**: *because, now that, since*</li><li>**contrast**: *although, even though, though*</li><li>**condition**: *if, only if, unless, whether or not, in that case, e.g.,* "When we were in Brazil, we went to Rio de Janeiro and Sao Paulo." "We went to Rio de Janeiro and Sao Paulo when we were in Brazil."</li></ul>(*There are many, many more subordinating conjunctions.)

SENTENCES

A sentence is a group of words that has a subject and predicate, and expresses a complete idea. A subject tells us what or whom the sentence is about and the predicate makes a statement about what the subject is or does. (In all the following examples, subjects are underlined and predicates italicized.)

Example sentence: The snow *falls quietly*	
Subject	The subject, or the topic of a sentence, consists of a noun or a pronoun and all the words that modify it. "The snow" is the subject in the above example. The simple subject is the main part of the subject. *Snow* is the simple subject.
Predicate	The predicate makes a statement or a comment about the subject and it consists of a verb and all the words that modify it; *falls quietly* is the predicate in the above example. The simple predicate is the main part of the predicate and is always the verb; *falls* is the simple predicate.
Compound subject	A subject that consists of two or more nouns or pronouns, e.g., Books and magazines *filled the room.*
Compound predicate	A predicate that contains more than one verb pertaining to the subject, e.g., The boys *walked and talked.*

Sentence Types

Subjects and predicates can be modified and combined in different ways to make simple, compound, or complex sentences.

Sentence Types	
Simple	A simple sentence, or independent clause, is a complete thought consisting of a subject and a predicate: The bus _was late._
Compound	A compound sentence consists of two independent clauses joined together by a coordinator (_and, or, nor, but, for, yet, so_): Tom _walked to the bus station,_ **and** he _took the bus._
Complex	A complex sentence is a sentence consisting of a dependent clause (a group of words with a subject and predicate that are not a complete thought) and an independent clause joined together using a subordinator (_although, after, when, because, since, while_): After I _write the report,_ I _will submit it to my teacher._

Sentence Purposes

Sentences serve different purposes. They can make a statement (declarative); ask a question (interrogative); give a command (imperative); or express a sense of urgency (exclamatory). Understanding the different purposes for sentences can help ELLs understand the relationship between what they write and the ideas they want to express.

Sentence Purpose	
Declarative	A declarative sentence makes a statement: "Anna will feed the dog."
Interrogative	An interrogative sentence asks a question: "Anna, have you fed the dog?"
Imperative	An imperative sentence gives a command: "Anna, please feed the dog."
Exclamatory	An exclamatory sentence expresses a sense of urgency: "Anna, go feed the dog right now!"

Constructing sentences involves combining words in grammatically correct ways to communicate the desired thought. Avoiding fragments and run-ons requires continual sentence analysis. The test of a complete sentence is: Does it contain a subject and predicate and express a complete idea?

ELLs often over-generalize that sentence fragments are short and complete sentences are long. When they truly understand what constitutes a sentence, they will realize that length has nothing to do with whether a sentence is complete or not.

For example:
- "He ran." is a complete sentence.
- "After the very funny story began" is a fragment.

To make these distinctions, learners must know the parts of speech and understand the difference between independent clauses and dependent clauses. Practice identifying independent clauses, dependent clauses, and phrases will help ELLs to write complete sentences.

Clauses and Phrases	
Independent clause	Independent clauses can stand alone or can be joined to other clauses.
Dependent clause	Dependent clauses contain at least one subject and one verb, but they cannot stand alone as a complete sentence. They are structurally dependent on the main clause.
Phrase	A phrase is a group of words that does not have a subject and a predicate and cannot stand alone. The most common types of phrases are: Prepositional: "in the room" Participial: "walking down the street" Infinitive: "to run"

Sentence Transformations

Sentences are transformed to add, delete, or permute informational content. There are many kinds of grammar. Chomsky proposed transformational grammar beginning in the 1950s. The term is still used to explain the relationships between the spoken word and its underlying meaning by distinguishing between sounds, words (and word parts), groups of words, and phrases. Sentences have a surface structure and an underlying structure according to generative grammarians. The rules that interpret the underlying structures and modify them to create the same surface structure are called **transformations**.

There are numerous possible transformations in the English language. Some of the most common ones used in ESOL teaching are listed below.

Sentence Transformations: ways in which the sentence adds, deletes, or permutes components	
Yes/no questions	**Sentences may be transformed into yes/no questions.** **auxiliary verb + subject + main verb + rest of sentence:** He lives in Chicago. Does he live in Chicago? Yes, he does. No, he doesn't.

Information questions	**Sentences may be transformed into information questions.** **question word + auxiliary verb + subject + main verb + rest of sentence:** Susan lives near Orlando. Where does Susan live? Near Orlando./She lives near Orlando. Will Julius be living alone in the house? How will Julius be living in the house? Alone./Julius will be living alone in the house.
Active voice to passive voice or vice versa	**Sentences may be changed from one voice to another voice.** I saw John. John was seen by me. John was being helped by me. I was helping John.
Indirect objects	**The word "to" (phrase marker) may be deleted.** I gave a cookie to him. I gave him a cookie. I mailed the article to the newspaper. I mailed the newspaper the article.
Imperatives	**The imperative or commands have no expressed subject.** You sit. You jump. Sit! Jump!
Negatives	**Linguists distinguish between two types of negation** **Affirmative sentences may be transformed into negative sentences where the whole sentence is negative.** Marion is happy. Marion is not happy. **Parts of sentences may be negative.** Juliana is happy. Juliana is unhappy.

Verb Tense

The basic English verb tenses are itemized below. Tense refers to any conjugated form expressing time, aspect, or mood. The charts omit the negative and interrogative forms.

Verb Tenses	Simple	Progressive	Perfect	Perfect progressive
Present	I write	I am writing	I have written	I have been writing
Past	I wrote	I was writing	I had written	I had been writing
Future	I will write	I will be writing	I will have written	I will have been writing

This table, of course, omits a number of forms that can be regarded as additional to the basic system:

- The intensive present: *I do write*
- The intensive past: *I did write*
- The habitual past: *I used to write*
- The "shall future": *I shall write*
- The "going-to future": *I am going to write*
- The "future in the past": *I was going to write*
- The conditional: *I would write*
- The perfect conditional: *I would have written*
- The subjunctive: *if I be writing, if I were writing.*

The term **discourse** refers to linguistic units composed of several sentences and is derived from the concept of "discursive formation" or communication that involves specialized knowledge of various kinds. Discourse plays a role in all spoken and written language. Discourse shapes the way language is transmitted and how we organize our thoughts. Conversations, arguments, or speeches are types of **spoken discourse**.

The structure of discourse varies among languages and traditions. For example, Japanese writing does not present the main idea at the beginning of an essay; rather, writing builds up to the main idea, which is presented or implied at the end of the essay. This structure is completely different from English writing, which typically presents the main idea or thesis at the beginning of an essay and repeats it at the end.

In addition to language and structure, topic—or focus—affects discourse. The discourse in various disciplines (such as feminist studies, cultural studies, and literary theory) approaches topics differently.

Discourse between speakers of English requires knowledge of certain protocols in addition to other aspects of spoken language. Speakers should have the necessary skills to maintain the momentum of a conversation, as well as to correct misunderstandings. Typical spoken discourse follows predictable patterns. For example, one person might say, "I saw a good movie last night." The other person would ask, "What was it about?" The first person then answers in a paragraph with a topic sentence: "It was about a bunch of guys who devised a plan to rob a casino." and then proceeds to fill in the details.

Vocal discourse varies significantly depending on context. People speak in different styles depending on who they are talking to and what the occasion demands. A candidate who is running for president and speaking to a group will use more formal speech than when having a casual conversation. The message conveyed may also vary, depending on whether the group is one of supporters or people who hold different political views. In either case, the candidate must make choices about how to organize what he or she says to ensure comprehension and to hold the audience's interest.

ELLs might initially practice set conversations to learn the patterns of English discourse. Practicing in pairs, using a question and answer format, gives both participants an opportunity to learn the structures of discourse as well as information about the other person or the other person's culture. Such practice also gives students practice with other language skills and can increase vocabulary. The teacher may provide a set of questions and learners can alternate asking and answering. Short skits that repeat a limited number of words also provide helpful practice. Allowing students time to converse informally, perhaps using suggested topics continues to reinforce speech patterns.

Polite discourse includes what is called "empty language" or perfunctory speech that has little meaning but is important in social exchanges. Frequently English speakers start a conversation by asking, "How are you?" even though they have no real interest in the other person's health. An appropriate response would be, "Fine," even if the person may not feel well. The exchange is simply a polite means of starting a conversation. Likewise, at the end of a discourse empty language is frequently employed: "It was good to see you." "Good to see you, too." This type of discourse is considered to be part of the Basic Interpersonal Communication Skills (**BICS**) that learners must acquire to function in social situations. It is generally less demanding than Cognitive Academic Language Proficiency (**CALP**), and allows learners to participate in informal conversations.

Written discourse ranges from the most basic grouping of sentences to the most complicated essays and stories. Regardless of the level, English writing demands certain structure patterns. A typical paragraph begins with a topic sentence, which states directly or indirectly the focus of the paragraph; adds supporting ideas and details; and ends with a concluding sentence that relates to the focus and either states the final thought on that topic or provides a transition to the next paragraph when there are more than one. As with spoken discourse, organization, tone, and word choice are critical to transferring thoughts successfully and maintaining interest.

As skills increase, paragraphs are combined into stories or essays. Each type of writing has specific components and structures. Story writing requires setting, plot, and character. Initially, following a chronological order is probably easiest for ELLs, but as learners become more skillful, other types of order should be practiced, such as adding descriptions in spatial order.

Teachers frequently rely on the proverbial three- or five-paragraph structure to teach essay writing because it provides a rigid structure for organizing and expanding ideas within a single focus. It mirrors the paragraph structure organizationally in that the first, or introductory, paragraph provides the main idea or focus of the essay; each body paragraph develops a supporting idea and adds details; and the concluding paragraph provides a summary or other type of conclusion that relates to the main idea or focus stated in the first paragraph. Obviously, no one considers such mechanical writing style to be the ultimate goal of essay writing. However, especially for ELLs, having a rigid structure teaches the basic organizational concept of English language essays. By offering strictly defined limits, the teacher reduces the number of variables to learn about essay writing. Starting with a blank page can be overwhelming to ELLs. Working within an organized structure enables learners to focus on developing each paragraph—a challenging enough task, when one considers the language skills required! As learners become better able to control their writing and sustain a focus, variations can be introduced and topics expanded.

Language proficiency requires both BICS and CALP. While they have clear distinctions, they also have underlying similarities that contribute to overall language learning. In addition, students should also recognize Common Underlying Proficiency (**CUP**). These are skills, ideas, and concepts that learners can transfer from their first language to their English learning. Similarities and differences between languages can both help learners comprehend and learn aspects of English.

American English usage is influenced by the social and regional situation of its users. Linguists have found that speakers adapt their pronunciation, vocabulary, grammar and sentence structure depending on the social situation. For example, the decision to use "ing" or "in'" at the end of a present participle depends on the formality of the situation. Speakers talking with their friends will often drop the "g" and use "–in'" to signal that the situation is more informal and relaxed. These variations are also related to factors such as age, gender, education, socioeconomic status, and personality.

We call this type of shift a "change in register," how language is used in a particular setting or for a particular purpose. People change their speech register depending on such sociolinguistic variables as

- Formality of situation
- Attitude towards topic
- Attitude towards listeners
- Relation of speaker to others

Changing speech registers may be completely subconscious for native speakers. For example, if a university professor takes his car in for servicing, the manner and speech he uses to communicate with the mechanic differs significantly from the manner and speech he uses to deliver a lecture. If he were to use a formal tone and academic vocabulary, the mechanic might think the professor was trying to put him down, or he might not understand what the professor was saying. Likewise, when the mechanic explains the mechanical diagnosis, he most likely chooses a simplified vocabulary rather than using completely technical language, or jargon, that the professor wouldn't understand. Using the jargon of a profession or field with which the listener is unfamiliar will likely make the listener feel stupid or inferior, and perhaps make him or her think that the speaker is inconsiderate.

Language registers are also used to deliberately establish a social identity. Hispanics deliberately refer to themselves as La Raza (the race) to imply dignity and pride for who they are and where they come from. Using a Spanish term when speaking English is called code switching. As a result, this term is becoming (or has become) a part of the American vocabulary. Symbolically it represents both the Hispanics' distinction and their integration into American culture.

ESOL teachers should be aware of these sociolinguistic functions of language and compare different social functions of language with their students. Knowing and being able to use appropriate registers allows learners to function more effectively in social situations. Learners must acquire the social, as well as the linguistic, aspects of American English. Sociolinguistic functions of a language are best acquired by using the language in authentic situations.

Sociolinguistic diversity, which is language variations based on regional and social differences, affects teachers' language attitudes and practices. Teachers must respect the validity of any group's or individual's language patterns, while at the same time teaching traditional English. Vernacular versions of English have well-established patterns and rules to support them. Making learners aware of language variations leads to increased interest in language learning and better ability to switch among one or more registers or dialects and standard English.

ELLs tend to adapt linguistic structures to their familiar culture, modifying specific concepts and practices. Teachers must identify these variations, call attention to them, and teach the appropriate English equivalent. The goal is not to eliminate linguistic diversity, but rather to enable learners to control their language use so that they can willfully use standard English *in addition to* their cultural variation. Various functional adaptations of English have great significance to the cultural groups that use them. Attempting to eliminate variations is not only futile, but raises hostility and reluctance to learn English. Stable, socially shared structures emerge from the summed effects of many individual communication practices Firmly ingrained language patterns serve a purpose within the community that uses them. Unique variations can arise in a school venue. New, nonstandard English words can represent a particular group's identity, or function as a means to solidify social relationships. As long as students recognize that a variation should not be used as if it were standard English, there should be no problem with its use.

Academic discourse refers to formal academic learning. This includes all of the four language skills: listening, reading, speaking, and writing. Academic learning is important in order for students to succeed in school. Cummins differentiated between two types of language proficiency: basic interpersonal communication skills (BICS) and cognitive academic language proficiency (CALP). According to research, an average student can acquire BICS within two to five years of language learning whereas CALP can take from four to seven years. A lot of factors are involved in the acquisition of CALP, such as age, language proficiency level, literacy in the first language, etc.

Academic discourse includes not only the knowledge of content-area vocabulary, but also the knowledge of various skills and strategies that are essential to successfully complete academic tasks in a mainstream classroom. It includes skills such as inferring, classifying, analyzing, synthesizing, and evaluating. Textbooks used in classrooms require abstract thinking relating to information that is context reduced. As students reach higher grades, they are required to think critically and apply this knowledge to solve problems.

Additionally, the language of academic discourse is complex for English language learners. With respect to reading and writing, complex grammatical structures are frequently found in academic discourse, which makes it challenging for the learners. Also, passive voice is normally used to present science and other subject-area textbooks. Similarly, the use of reference, pronouns, modals, etc, is a common feature of academic discourse which might cause problems for ESL learners. All of the language features of academic discourse help to convey the intended meaning of the author; therefore, it is necessary to explicitly teach these language features to students in order for them to become skilled readers and writers.

Furthermore, genre is an important aspect of academic discourse. Each genre employs a style of writing that is unique to itself. The organization of a text structure differs according to the purpose of the author, for example, mystery versus romance. Likewise, in academic reading, students come across multiple texts that vary in organization and style according to the purpose of the author, and the audience in question. Students need to understand the different features of multiple texts to become efficient readers. With respect to writing, students need to determine the purpose of their writing, for example, argumentative writing versus story writing.

In short, explicit instruction of these language skills—grammar, vocabulary, and genre—should be provided to students to help them learn academic discourse in order for them to succeed in a school setting.

Oral discourse analysis is often referred to as conversational analysis. In oral discourse, the emphasis is on the behavior of the participants and social constraints such as politeness and face-saving phenomena. Oral discourse analysis is concerned with who initiates the conversation, turn-taking, how not to interrupt, and who speaks next.

Written discourse is generally analyzed for how the text hangs together. **Cohesion** is the "surface" characteristics of the semantic relationships between the elements of the text. **Coherence** is the deeper meaning of the logical elements of the text. Other elements of written discourse include theme, anaphora, topic progression, and grammatical choices at the clausal level.

Skill 4.4   Use of semantics and pragmatics in determining meaning in connected discourse

Semantics encompasses the meaning of individual words, as well as combinations of words. Native speakers use their language to function in their daily lives at all levels. Through experience, they know the effects of intonation, connotation, and synonyms. This is not true of foreign speakers. In an ESOL class, we are trying to teach as quickly as possible what the native speaker already knows. The objectives of beginning ESOL lesson plans should deliberately build a foundation that will enable students to meet more advanced objectives.

Teaching within a specific context helps students to understand the meaning of words and sentences. When students can remember the context in which they learned words and recall how the words were used, they retain that knowledge and can compare it with different applications of the same words as they are introduced.

Using words in a variety of contexts helps students reach deeper understanding of the words. They can then guess at new meanings that are introduced in different contexts. For example, the word "conduct" can be taught in the context of conducting a meeting or an investigation. Later the word "conductor" can be used in various contexts that demonstrate some similarity but have distinctly different uses of the word, such as a conductor of electricity, the conductor of a train, the conductor of an orchestra, and so forth.

Second language learners must learn to translate words and sentences that they already understand in their primary language into the language they wish to acquire. This can be a daunting task because of the many ways meaning is created in English. Voice inflection, variations of meaning, variations of usage, and emphasis are some of the factors that affect meaning. The lexicon of language includes the stored meaning and contextual meaning from word association, as well as knowledge of pronunciation, grammar, and morphemes.

interpretation →

Pragmatics is the study of how the context impacts the interpretation of language. Situations dictate language choice, body language, the degree of intimacy, and how meaning is interpreted. For example, when customers walk into a bar and sit down on stools, they expect a bartender will ask them several questions: "What would you like to drink?" and "Would you like to start a tab?" This sequence of events and cues is a typical pattern of interaction in a bar. Pragmatic knowledge provides the customer with a set of expectations for the flow of events. Pragmatic knowledge sets customer expectations. Typically, people in a bar expect a certain level of social exchange that allows congeniality without intrusiveness. They expect to receive a certain level of service, and to use a particular level of manners. These types of exchanges are fairly universal in bars, but would be completely inappropriate in a more formal setting; for example, when conversing with the president of a corporation.

Gestures, the appropriate distance between speakers, seating arrangements, nodding and shaking of the head, signs, and touch are all examples of nonverbal pragmatic conventions. These elements are different in different cultures and may be taught.

In the ESL classroom, pragmatics can be illustrated and practiced by repeating the same situation in different contexts. For example, students can write or act out how they would explain why they failed a test to three different people: their best friend, their teacher, and their parent. With a little imagination, different scenarios can be chosen that pique student interest and make learning fun. For example, explain an embarrassing event in different contexts, such as in front of a boy/girl you want to impress, a close friend, and an authority figure. For students with very low language skills, pantomime can encourage participation, teach the concept, and create an opportunity for using language to describe what has happened.

For students from other cultures, pragmatics involving nonverbal cues and body language can be confusing. It is the teacher's responsibility to be sensitive to these different behaviors and acknowledge them when they become obvious in the classroom, and to guide students to adopt behaviors appropriate to their audience, purpose, and setting.

Students may be unaware that others feel uncomfortable because they are standing too close or not making eye contact. These situations are very common examples of cultural differences in nonverbal communication. In some cultures, it is considered impolite to look a teacher in the eye—exactly the opposite behavior expected of North Americans! The problem could be addressed directly by discussing appropriate behaviors in different cultures, perhaps by focusing on behavior appropriate to the teacher as a model.

Other examples of nonverbal communication are gestures, tone, volume, stress, and intonation. Appropriate use varies in different social settings. All students (and not just ELLs) need to learn the appropriate voice volume for different settings such as the library, hall, gymnasium, supermarket, and movie theater. An appropriate correction for young children would be to ask all the class members to use their "inside" voices and not their "outside" (playground) voices when speaking in the classroom.

Skill 4.5   Major theorists in sociolinguistics (e.g., Labov, Fishman, Hymes, Bernstein) and knowledge of sociolinguistic concepts (e.g., dialect diversity in English; factors affecting language variation, register, and style; intercultural differences in communication styles)

Sociolinguistics is the study of how social conditions influence the use of language. Social factors such as ethnicity, religion, gender, status, age, and education all play a role in how individuals use language. Dialects differ depending on these and other factors. Sociolinguistics tries to understand the relationship between language and social elements. Different dialects, or how language is spoken, are frequently referred to today as varieties of a language. Varieties of a language may be considered separate languages if there is a strong literary, religious, or other tradition.

MAJOR THEORISTS

Labov
Known for his work in the area of **dialects**, specifically African American Vernacular English where he proved this dialect a distinct variety of English with its own rules, syntax, and grammar.

Fishman
Studied how language evolved and changed over time. His work with Gaelic, Welsh, and Yiddish helped identify the forces in society which may help languages survive. Fishman differed from Ferguson's (1959) original concept of **disglossia**. He believed there could be more than two varieties of language within in a disglossic community. He also believed that all kinds of language varieties which show functional distribution in a language community can be referred to as disglossia. Thus, disglossia ranges from the use of separate dialects to the use of separate languages.

Hymes
Hymes early work focused on the relationship between language and its social context. His notion of **communicative competence** was devised (using the SPEAKING acronym below) to study how people talked. Hymes believed that native speaker's competence to speak their language is not sufficient to explain their ability to use grammatically correct forms. He felt that the native speaker also knows when and where to use them, leading to communicative competence.

Hymes' model of discourse analysis explaining the relationship between society, culture and language may be remembered using the acronym **SPEAKING:**

S- setting and scene
P- participants (speaker and audience)
E- ends, purpose, goals
A- act sequence (form and order of event)
K- key (cues that establish the tone, manner or spirit)
I- instrumentalities (forms and styles of speech)
N-norms (social rules)
G- genre (kind of speech act or event)

Bernstein

Bernstein's early work concentrated on two codes used in language: the restricted code and the elaborated code stirred considerable controversy. The **restricted code** is used among speakers with similar backgrounds who share similar background knowledge and experiences. This code is more restricted as the users tend to use certain grammatical features with less frequency because the speakers understand each other's assumptions, perspectives, feelings, and ways of speaking. Since speakers have similar assumptions and understanding of topics each word acts as an index with complex meanings that leave much left unsaid but understood by the listener.

The **elaborated code** is used with speakers who do not share the same background or experiences. This code is more elaborate in the use of grammar structures, pronouns, amount of language used to express ideas because the speakers are not as familiar with the backgrounds, experiences, assumptions, outlooks, perspectives etc. of each other. Therefore, they use more words, phrases, forms to express meaning.

Bernstein found that low economic status children in Britain showed use of only the restricted code while middle class children showed greater ability to use both codes. He claimed that there are two factors which contribute to the development of the different codes. One is the nature of the socializing agencies (family, peers, school and work) and the second one is the values within the system. His early work on codes has led to studies in how educational knowledge is constructed.

Historical variation may occur in the sound system, the grammar, or the lexicon. It may be a gradual change in the pronunciation of a word, or it may be abrupt, as in the case of pidginization of the language when contact with a new culture occurs. It is beyond anyone's control, but language is constantly changing. In the words of H. L. Mencken, "A living language is like a man suffering incessantly from small haemorrhages, and what it needs above all else is constant transactions of new blood from other tongues. The day the gates go up, that day it begins to die."

France is a prime example of a country that has tried to keep its language "pure." In spite of tremendous efforts, the French language has evolved. It has acquired new terms for twentieth- and twenty-first-century technology and experiences. It has been modified by immigrants who have moved to France. Living languages are simply not static.

Social language is different from **academic language.** The languages are used in different contexts and for different purposes. Their vocabularies are distinct. Structures and grammar may also be distinct. Social language is generally used with peers, in relaxed and informal contexts. Academic language is often used to convey scholarly concepts with concern for accuracy, objectivity, and dispassionate comment.

The United States has experienced disparate social influences, which accounts for the substantial differences between American and other varieties of English, even British English from which American English originated. Ralph Waldo Emerson said, "The English language is the sea which receives tributaries from every region under heaven." Most obvious of these tributaries has been the continuous flow of immigrants who have brought their customs and languages to the United States. Each culture contributes new words, and new immigrants continue to change the language today.

Language is influenced by the **geography** of the land in which it is spoken. Imagine the different words needed to describe the geographical features of the snowy, icy northern countries and the words needed to describe the lands of the harsh, barren deserts. Nomadic peoples in these areas use different vocabularies with words not easily translated because the people living in other regions have no concepts upon which to base the words.

Wars have also added words to our language. During World War II, people began to use words and phrases such as *flak, blitz, R & R, black market, pin-up, mushroom cloud,* and *fallout.* During the Korean War, *chopper* and *brainwashing* came into use. During the Vietnam era, *napalm, friendly fire, search-and-destroy mission,* and *the domino theory* entered the language. The Iraq War has added *the green zone, al-Qaeda,* and *weapons of mass destruction.* Wars also give new meanings to old words, such as *embedded,* which in the context of Iraq means journalists who join army units.

Contemporary culture changes language significantly. Advertisers have such great success that brand names come to represent entire categories of products, such as *Kleenex* for tissue, *Xerox* for photocopy, *Hoover* for vacuum cleaner, and *Coke* for cola. People pick up and use phrases from popular TV shows: *Yabadabadoo; like, cool, man; and D'oh!* Other cultural trends, such as the drug culture, sports, and fads add new words to the language.

Political rhetoric also influences language. We hear sports metaphors (a success referred to as a homerun); war metaphors (victories or defeats); and business metaphors (ending up in the red or the black). Politicians like to "send a message" to enemies, political rivals, or the American people. Candidates like to be "the candidate of change" or "the education candidate."

Technology and science may have changed language more than any other factor in the past century. An estimated five hundred thousand technical and scientific terms have been added to English. Many of these words affect our daily lives. Fifty years ago, people didn't routinely use computers, cell phones, the Internet, or satellite dishes. They hadn't had an MRI or wondered if genetically modified organisms (GMOs) were safe to eat.

Text messaging, particularly among young people, has created a kind of shorthand variation of English: *CUL8R* means "see you later"; *BRB* means "be right back"; and *TTYL* means "talk to you later." ESL teachers might be surprised at how adroit their students are with technological language. Students who make English-speaking friends and want to adapt to U.S. culture will quickly learn this new language.

The merging of languages into English has contributed to the inconsistencies and exceptions to rules that make the language so difficult to learn. It has also increased the number of words one must learn to communicate in English. We can only be certain that English will continue to change and language will continue to be vital in new forms.

Work-related language (**jargon**) is often different from the language of the general public. To the professionals using it, jargon may be a kind of shorthand that makes long explanations unnecessary. Consider the multitude of terms used to refer to those learning English as an additional language (e.g., English as a Second Language students, English as a Foreign Language students, English Language Learners, and those with Limited English Proficiency) to name a few. Teachers may be referred to as TESOL, ESL, or EFL teachers, or simply bilingual teachers. The general public would be hard-pressed to understand the distinctions made by professionals using these terms.

Choice of language for a particular discourse refers to **register**. Register varies with many factors including context, age, gender, and culture, level of education, social class, and vocation. British linguist Michael Halliday first defined the broadened term of register as three factors leading to variations in the formality between the participants:

- **Field of discourse:** A reference to the subject matter being discussed
- **Mode of discourse:** Speaking or writing, and the choice of format
- **Manner of discourse:** A reference to the social relations between the participants

COMPETENCY 5.0   UNDERSTAND SHELTERED/STRUCTURED ENGLISH IMMERSION (SEI) THEORIES, PROGRAMS, AND INSTRUCTIONAL APPROACHES FOR ENGLISH LANGUAGE LEARNERS

Skill 5.1   Knowledge of research (e.g., by Lambert, Ramirez, Gersten, Rossell & Baker) on effective second-language immersion programs

The Bilingual Education Act, Title VII of the Elementary and Secondary Education Act of 1965 created an energetic debate on bilingual education programs. Second language acquisition consists of three distinct programs: immersion (also called submersion), English as a Second Language (ESL), and bilingual education. Immersion programs have tried, with varying degrees of success, to engage our linguistically diverse population in mainstream U.S. education programs. In this program model, students are expected to "sink or swim". They are given no native language linguistic support and are expected to perform at a level equivalent to native speakers. The main goal of immersion programs is that students acquire English as soon as possible through continuous and constant submersion within the language (Brisk; Baker & Jones, 1998).

Lambert: Proponent of Transitional
The Two-Way Bilingual Education Model is based on strong content and other academic achievement in both languages. Teachers use hands-on activities, thematic units, peer interaction, multiple clues, and whole language approaches to teach ELLs and English native speakers content in a language that is not their heritage language. The goals of such programs are to provide students with ample exposure to both languages and allow them to progress academically in both languages while appreciating another culture (CAL, 1999). While the goals are the same, the methods used to achieve these goals may vary by:

- **Content:** Social studies and math are taught in French, while math, arts, and music are taught in English.
- **Time:** Instruction is given in each language on alternate days
- **Person:** One teacher uses Navajo and one teacher uses English
- **Language development methods:** Start at 90% instruction in native language (so 90-10, 80-20, 70-30, 60-40, 50-50...) Used in the Amigos Program in Cambridge, Massachusetts (reported on by Cabazon, Lambert & Hall, 1992).
  - Students were basically satisfied with the program.
  - Students did not believe that their academic progress had been hampered.
  - Investigators believe that student perceptions of a program are essential to the evaluation of a program's effectiveness.

Lambert (1990) also distinguished between Second Language Learning and Foreign Language Learning, citing differences in:

- Training, goals, orientations, and their practice are directed at different users.

- There is a more serious demand than by those being educated for higher levels of competence in foreign language and second languages then usually occurs in school-based programs.
- Time constraints limit the amount of time spent on English language development if it interferes with math, sciences, humanities, and social science.

Ramirez: Proponent of Late Exit

The U. S. Department of Education (1991) reported the results of a national longitudinal study, informally known as the Ramirez Report after its primary investigator. Data was collected from over 2,300 Spanish-speaking students in 554 classrooms (K-6) in New York, New Jersey, Florida, Texas and California (Samway & McKeon, 1999 in Cruz). The study compared Structured English Immersion programs to two types of bilingual programs. Investigators observed the classrooms over a period of four years to verify the presence of hypothesized differences in the programs. In reality, the only hypothesized difference found to occur in actual practice was the percentage of instructional time teachers taught in English compared to Spanish (Baker, 1998)

The study concluded that students in immersion and early-exit transitional programs progressed at the same rate as students from the general population. While the students in the immersion and early-exit programs did not fall behind other students, neither were they able to bridge the gap between the two groups. Cummins & Genzuk (1991) stated that the study provides support for the belief that primary language skill development facilitates the acquisition of English language skills.

Gersten: Proponent of Early Exit

In 2000, Gersten, Russell, Baker, and Scott published research gathered over a four year period using the qualitative multivocal method of Ogawa & Malen (1991). They conducted five work groups consisting of researchers, teachers, administrators, psychologists, and staff developers. Their twin goals were to understand what these professionals viewed as recurrent problems in instruction and what terms practitioners used to describe current practices (2000). Their findings indicate that:

- Language growth and academic growth are difficult to distinguish between and should be more closely studied.
- English- language development in bilingual education and bilingual special education is a major problem, especially for special education students because they cannot keep up.
- A good English-language program should include three components:
  - Development of both fluency and proficiency in English social and academic communication.
  - More high quality study of the formal, grammatical aspects of the English language.
  - Emphasis on learning academic content.
- A drastic increase in the quality and quantity of instructional intervention studies of English language learners, including studies with ELL students with disabilities.

- New research in the field needs to be well-designed and valid.
- The professionals' work resulted in a set of principles and practices that will be useful in defining best practices.

In other work, Gersten and Baker (2001) have called for teachers to reduce their English language demands when students are challenged cognitively, and reduce cognitive content when students are learning English.

Rossell & Baker
Rossell and Baker released a study in 1996 in which they evaluated the effectiveness of bilingual education programs. They selected only 72 (of 300) programs to be methodologically acceptable and concluded that little evidence exists that bilingual education works.

Many theorists, including Cummins and Krashen, have challenged their findings. Cummins claimed that when they compared transitional bilingual education (TBE) with structured immersion in reading performance, no differences were found in 17% and in 83%, structured immersion in English was superior (Cummins, 1998). Krashen questioned the rigor of many studies included in their evaluation, claiming they included as methodologically acceptable all unfavorable to bilingual education and many unpublished in professional literature (Krashen in Crawford, 1998). In addition, Rossell and Baker used a narrative technique (vs. meta-analysis of numerous variables) counting votes for or against bilingual education (Dunkel in Crawford, 1998).

Skill 5.2   Characteristics and goals of effective sheltered/structured English immersion Programs

The major models of ESOL programs differ, depending on the sources consulted. However, general consensus recognizes the following program models with different instructional methods.

Immersion Education Models
In these programs, instruction is initiated in the student's non-native language, using the second language as the medium of instruction for both academic content and the second language. Two of these models strive for full bilingualism: one is for language majority students and the other is for language minorities.

- **English Language Development (ELD) or English as a Second Language (ESL) Pull-out:** This category includes various approaches to teaching English to non-native speakers. In 1997 TESOL standards defined these approaches by an intent to teach the ELL to communicate in social settings, engage in academic tasks, and use English in socially and culturally appropriate ways. Three well-known approaches to ELD or ESL are:

- o **Grammar-based ESL:** Teaches <u>about</u> the language, stressing its structure, functions, and vocabulary through rules, drills, and error correction.
- o **Communication-based ESL:** Instruction in English that emphasizes <u>using </u>the language in meaningful contexts. There is little stress on correctness in the early stages and more emphasis on comprehensible input in the early stages to foster communication and lower anxiety when risk-taking.
- o **Content-based ESL:** Instruction in English that attempts to develop language skills and prepare ELLs to study grade-level content material in English. Emphasis on language, but with graded introduction to content areas, vocabulary and basic concepts.

- **Structured English immersion:** The goal is English proficiency. ELLs are pulled out for structured instruction in English so that subject matter is comprehensible. Used with sizeable groups of ELLs who speak the same language and are in the same grade level or with a diverse population of language minority students. There is little or no L1 language support. Teachers use sheltered instructional techniques and have strong receptive skills in the students' native or heritage language.

- **Submersion with primary language support:** The goal is English proficiency. Bilingual teachers or aides support the minority students in each grade level who are ELLs. In small groups, the ELLs are tutored by reviewing the content areas in their primary language. The teachers use the L1 to support English content classes; ELLs achieve limited literacy in L1.

- **Canadian French immersion (language-majority students):** The goal is bilingualism in French (L2) and English (L1). The targeted population is the language-majority. Students are immersed in the L2 for the first 2 years using sheltered language instruction and then English L1 is introduced. The goal is for all students of the majority language (English) to become fluent in L2 (French).

- **Indigenous language immersion (endangered languages, such as Navajo):** The goal is bilingualism; the program is socially, linguistically and cognitively attuned to the native culture and community context. This method supports endangered minority language, and develops academic skills in minority language and culture as well as in the English language and predominate culture.

- **Self-contained:** This method consists of monolingual English instruction using ESL methods to teach oral and written English and to foster cognitive development. This is a strategic option for schools not staffed with a sufficient number of bilingual teachers. An ESL classroom instructs students in English but remains sensitive to their home language and cultures.

- **Newcomer centers/programs:** These centers are designed to temporarily help newcomers to the U.S. adjust to both the educational system and the social environment. These centers/programs differ tremendously in their structure and set-up. Some are part of the regular school system and others are self-contained. While the centers are an ad-hoc response to local education needs, they share a dedication to helping LEP newcomer students transition to the American school system as quickly as possible, and also share an educational approach which recognizes the importance of acquiring English language skills, but recognizes that language skills are but one of the necessary skills necessary in the transition process.

Research findings suggest that there are several characteristics of effective programs for language minority groups:

- Supportive whole-school contexts (Lucas, Henze, & Donato, 1990; Tikunoff et al., 1991)
- High expectations for language minority groups supported by active learning environments that are academically challenging (Collier, 1992; Lucas, Henze, & Donato; Pease-Alvarez, Garcia, & Espinosa, 1991)
- Intensive staff development programs designed to assist ALL teachers in providing effective instruction to language minority students (Lucas, Henze, & Donato, 1990; Tikunoff et al., 1991)
- Expert instructional leaders and teachers (Lucas, Henze, & Donato, 1990; Pease-Alvarez, Garcia & Espinosa, 1991; Tikunoff et al, 1991)
- Emphasis on functional communication between teacher and students and among fellow students (Garcia, 1991)
- Organization of the instruction of basic skills and academic content around thematic units (Garcia, 1991)
- Frequent student interaction through the use of collaborative learning techniques (Garcia, 1991)
- Teachers with a high commitment of the educational success of all their students (Garcia, 1991)
- Principals supportive of their instructional staff and of teacher autonomy while maintaining an awareness of district policies on curriculum and academic accountability (Garcia, 1991)
- Involvement of majority and minority parents in formal parent support activities (Garcia, 1991)

(Adapted from Rennie, J., 1993. ESL and Bilingual Program Models)

Skill 5.3   Features and theoretical bases of methods of second language instruction that can be used to promote language and content learning in SEI classrooms (e.g., Natural Approach, communicative language teaching, integrated language teaching, Cognitive Academic Language Learning Approach [CALLA], sheltered content teaching)

The following language learning theories support specific instructional strategies. Many of these theories overlap in theory and in practice.

THEORY: IN ORDER FOR THE L2 LEARNER TO BEGIN PRODUCTION IN THE TARGET LANGUAGE (TL), THE FOLLOWING PRINCIPLES MUST BE OBSERVED AND IMPLEMENTED

- During the silent period (when learners listen, instead of speaking), the instructors must use comprehensible input, corresponding to the learners' level of understanding in the TL.
- Attempts to speak and produce language on the part of the L2 learner, will gradually occur.
- The class curriculum must be aligned with specific speech production skills, i.e., instead of a linear-grammatical approach, instruction should be topically-centered, such as nonsequential lessons on weather, things found in a house, how to tell time, etc.

Strategy: The Natural Approach

T. Terrell and S. Krashen are the researchers behind the most comprehensive CBA/CBL approach: the "Natural Approach." The underlying assumption is that any learner of any age has the ability to receive comprehensible speech input and determine its pattern, without someone else having to spell it out for them. According to Terrell & Krashen, the approach involves large amounts of comprehensible input, whether it is situational, from visual aids/cues, or grammatical. This input is respectful of "the initial preproduction period, expecting speech to emerge not from artificial practice, but from motivated language use, progressing from early single-word responses up to more and more coherent discourse" (Celce-Murcia, 1991). He also maintains that being grammatically correct is not as important as the learner enjoying the learning process. Critics of Terrell maintain that by not correcting the learner's errors early on, fluency is achieved at the expense of accuracy.

THEORY: LEARNERS NEED NOT ONLY INPUT, BUT OUTPUT: IN ORDER TO LEARN A LANGUAGE, THEY MUST USE IT. CLT EMPHASIZES THE LEARNER AS AN INDIVIDUAL, THE VIEW OF LANGUAGE WHICH INCLUDES COMMUNICATIVE AND SOCIAL FACTORS IN ADDITION TO THE LINGUISTIC ONE

Strategy: Communicative Language Teaching (CLT) Emphasis is on:
There are many models of CLT which include most, if not all, of the following elements in varying degrees:

← focuses on fluency

- Appropriacy, not correctness
- Use, not usage
- Value (contextual, pragmatic meaning), not signification (meaning)
- Utterance, not sentence
- Illocutionary Act (defined in terms of function), not proposition (specific request or statement, does not have to be interpreted to have significance)
- Coherence (describes how a text hangs together, makes sense as ideas are clearly and logically stated), not coherence (formal features of a text which unite text at a linguistic level, e.g. pronouns, linking words, etc.)
- Communicative abilities (e.g. speaking, listening), not linguistic skills (e.g. speaking and hearing)
- Lexis should be the basis of CLT, not grammar
- Task-based learning
- Self-directed learning, not teacher-center classroom
- Learning to learn, i.e. teacher trains students in learning techniques
- Learner generated syllabus, i.e. learning communicative and linguistic skills needed to conduct real-world tasks

Learner autonomy is another feature of CLT. This feature encourages the ELL to gradually outgrow the need for a teacher by becoming more self-aware, self-reliant, and better able to learn directly from the experience (Trim, 1981).

THEORY: LANGUAGE LEARNERS WILL LEARN AUTHENTIC LANGUAGE AND GAIN A TRUER PICTURE OF THE COMPLEXITIES AND RICHNESS OF ENGLISH WHEN USED AS A REAL MEANS OF INTERACTING AND SHARING AMONG PEOPLE

Strategy: Integrated Language Teaching
The two main types of integrated language teaching are Content-Based Instruction and Task-Based Instruction. Both of these approaches require students to use language authentically to obtain information and to communicate information. Content-based instruction requires students to practice all the language skills in a highly integrated, communicative way while learning content (Oxford, 2001). The three main models of content-based instruction are:

- **Theme-based models:** Language skills are integrated in the study of themes or broad topics (e.g. drug abuse, recycling, homelessness)
- **Adjunct model:** Language and content courses are taught separately but closely coordinated
- **Sheltered model:** English is simplified to ELL's level of proficiency while teaching content. (Oxford, 2001)

Task-based learning is another way of achieving Integrated Language Teaching. Students are guided through tasks (Prabhu, 1987) formulated so that they are as realistic as possible. Three main trends in tasks are:

- **Communicativeness:** Learning is achieved through activities promoting real conversation between learners.
- **Tasks:** Learners who use language in a meaningful way to carry out tasks will learn language.
- **Meaningfulness:** Learners need to find meaning in the task for the learning tasks to be most effective.

THEORY: WHEN LEARNERS ARE INSTRUCTED THROUGH CONTENT-BASED INSTRUCTION SUCH AS MATHEMATICS, SCIENCE, SOCIAL STUDIES ETC., THEY TEND TO ACHIEVE A MUCH HIGHER PROFICIENCY LEVEL IN THE TL, THAN IF THEY WERE ONLY INSTRUCTED IN THE TL THROUGH ESL METHODS

Strategy: The Cognitive Academic Language Learning Approach (CALLA) Integrates the Following Tenets:

- The L2 learners' actual grade level in the main subject areas of mathematics, science, and social studies etc., should be the deciding factor for content.
- The L2 learners should be exposed to and gradually acquire the specific language used when studying in the subject areas, such as: add this column of numbers, determine "x" in this algebraic problem, identify the properties of this cell, etc.
- The L2 learners should be encouraged to use higher level cognitive processes, such as application, analysis and synthesis.

The CALLA teacher needs to first introduce basic literacy skills. If possible, these should be introduced in the native or heritage language of the child. For older students, the Language Experience Approach has proven effective. Another technique to use with older students is to have them read such everyday items as signs, menus, ads, and recipes because there is an immediate association with these materials and the need to learn to read (Chamot & O'Malley, 1994).

- **Creating illustrated autobiographies:** ("All about Me" or "The Story of My Life") can help ease ELLs into the academic challenges of a new school and culture. Students use as much English as they can and draw pictures to illustrate other points. This is an integrative activity because ELLs are not singled out, but are part of the group.

- **Dialogue journals:** Can be used with students of all ages. Provide all students with blank journals and allow them to draw or write in the language of their choice. The instructor should respond to the journals periodically. Journals are an excellent way to develop a personal relationship with the students while at the same time introducing literacy to the class.
- **Themes:** Such as "Where We Were Born" or "Family Origins" make good starting points to bring in home cultures and activate prior knowledge of all students.

(Adapted from Peregoy and Boyle, 2008)

THEORY: STUDENTS CAN LEARN CONTENT WHILE DEVELOPING THEIR ENGLISH LANGUAGE SKILLS

Strategy: Sheltered Content Teaching

In sheltered content teaching, students from diverse linguistic backgrounds are grouped together allowing teachers to instruct content through English adapted to the proficiency level of the students. Emphasis is on content though English language learning is also expected. California's Specifically Designed Academic Instruction in English (S.D.A.I.E.) is one example of this type of instruction. Sheltered content teaching—which is based upon the theories of Krashen (comprehensible input and affective environment) and Cummins (Basic Interpersonal Communication Skills—BICS and Cognitive Academic Language Proficiency--CALP) are indispensible components of Sheltered Content Teaching.

Some of the features of Sheltered Content Teaching would be:

- Comprehensible input
- Assessing prior knowledge
- Scaffolding
- Hands-on activities
- Visual clues (realia, word lists, pictures, models, gestures, body language)
- Cooperative learning
- Reduced language demands (teachers monitor their syntax, rate of speech, and language structures)
- Cultural affirmation and multicultural appreciation
- Graphic organizers
- Active learning with higher order thinking skills
- Teacher as a facilitator of learning

THEORY: IF THE INSTRUCTIONAL ENVIRONMENT FOR L2 LEARNERS IS CHARACTERIZED BY HIGH EXPECTATIONS FOR SPEAKING CORRECTLY, TOTAL MEMORIZATION OF GRAMMATICAL RULES AND VOCABULARY, AS WELL AS CONSTANT ERROR CORRECTION, THE L2 LEARNER WILL QUICKLY LOSE MOTIVATION TO CONTINUE THE LEARNING PROCESS

Strategy: Total Physical Response (TPR)

A "command-driven" instructional technique developed by the psychologist James Asher. TPR is a useful tool in the early developmental stage of second language acquisition, as well as for LEP students without any previous exposure to the English. The main tenet of TPR is that input is very comprehensible, in the form of commands and gestures and is also fun for the L2 learner. Asher supports this theory with the idea that the process mirrors the process that young children use when acquiring their primary language: children gradually develop both their awareness and attempts to communicate, until listening comprehension skills have reached a comfortable level. At this point, the child will begin to speak. Through TPR, instructors interact with students by way of commands/gestures, and the students respond with a physical response. TPR emphasizes listening rather than speaking; and, students are encouraged to speak only when they feel ready.

DOMAIN III   SECOND-LANGUAGE AND CONTENT LEARNING

COMPETENCY 6.0   UNDERSTAND STRATEGIES FOR PROMOTING AND ASSESSING ENGLISH LANGUAGE LEARNERS' ORAL LANGUAGE SKILLS AND COMMUNICATIVE LANGUAGE DEVELOPMENT

Skill 6.1   Strategies and activities for developing English language learners' communicative language skills (e.g., aural comprehension, listening and speaking vocabularies, knowledge of Standard English, listening and speaking for different purposes) and communicative competence in English

Language study using authentic language and the uses of language have become the watchwords in language acquisition. Theorists now believe that language use is the proper goal of language studies and that it should be studied in context instead of in isolated sentences which provide examples of only a specific grammar point or structure. In the move away from de-contextualized, graded textbooks, researchers encourage the study of discourse above the sentence level.

Teachers need to provide a wide range of materials, including educational technology (cassettes, video, computers, and CD-ROMs) to create a language- rich environment, believed to be the key to comprehensible input and high motivation.

And finally, all the four language skills—listening, speaking, reading and writing -- should be practiced at all levels. One way of achieving the practice of all four skills, while using authentic language, is to incorporate task-based activities into the instruction (1985), defining a task as "an activity or action which is carried out as a result of processing or understanding language."

The teacher must use a variety of methods to encourage students to use the new language rather than focusing only on comprehension. These can include activities such as the following, in which the objective is to learn the names of classroom objects:

- TPR activities, in which the student obeys a command ("Hold up a pencil") or displays a response on a slate or 3 x 5 card ("Draw a computer mouse").
- Duet reading (the students and teacher read aloud together at the same time).
- Races (each team sends up a runner who must touch whatever classroom object the teacher names before the other team's runner).
- Team drawing on the chalkboard ("Draw a classroom with a flag above the desk. Now draw a wastebasket beside the desk," etc.).
- Singing, rated as the single easiest way to remember new vocabulary.

- Cooperative learning tasks, in which each student has one piece of information and must get other information from classmates as well as share what he/she has with them.

Ellis (1994: 596-598) concluded that two-way exchanges of information show more benefits:

on test

 - Two-way tasks require more negotiation of meaning.
- ELLs usually produce more complex and more target-like language when they have sufficient time to plan their responses.
- Closed tasks (those with one single, correct solution) produce more negotiation work than those which have no predetermined solution.

With respect to listening skills, Ur (1996) lists some of the occasions on which we listen and appropriately respond:

- Interviews
- Instructions
- Loudspeaker announcements
- Radio news
- Committee meetings
- Shopping encounters
- Theater
- Telephone
- Lessons or lectures
- Conversation and gossip
- Television
- Story-telling

Most of these situations use language that is informal and spontaneous. In the classroom, teachers are training ELLs for real-life listening situations. Bearing this in mind, the most useful types of activities are those where the listener (ELL) is asked to listen to genuinely informal talk instead of the typical written text. The speaker should be visible to the listener and there should be direct speaker-listener interaction. Finally, there should be only one exposure to the text, as in real-life the listener will rarely have the opportunity to have the text "replayed."

The tasks themselves should be presented in such a way that the ELL can use his or her previous knowledge to anticipate outcomes. Saying "You are going to hear a husband and wife discussing summer vacation plans" is far more useful than merely stating, "Listen to the passage..." Also, ELLs should be given a task to complete as they listen (e.g., listen for information about where they are planning to go, mark this on their maps). Finally, ELLs should be permitted to answer the questions as they hear the information and not wait until the end.
(Adapted from Ur, 1996)

In recent years, the teaching of speaking skills has moved away from a focus on accuracy toward a focus on fluency and communicative effectiveness. This has affected the kinds of activities used by the teachers in the classroom. These communicative activities promote students' abilities to understand and communicate real information. It also provides opportunities for them to engage in interaction that is as close as possible to real life situations.

The selection of appropriate activities depends a lot on the level of the learners. For example, the beginning level students need form-controlled practice and drills to move to more communicative activities. On the other hand, advanced learners may be asked to engage in less structured activities on their own. Following are the examples of the kinds of activities that could promote speaking skills.

Linguistically Structured Activities

Despite recent claims, a focus on accuracy is considered important for language learners. Controlled activities can be provided with a context, so that they have some of the elements of a communicative activity. This would help the beginning-level student focus on accurate structure within a communicative context. An example of this is the *structured interview* where students question and answer each other, exchanging real information, while at the same time repeating and producing specific structures (e.g., yes, no, or "wh" questions).

Some language games can also provide students with controlled practice. However, it is important to model the language structures for beginning students. These and other games help students focus on and repeat specific structures as well as perform natural "authentic" tasks.

Participation Activities

Participation activities involve students in participating in some communication activity in a "natural" setting. One of these activities is the guided discussion, through which the teacher introduces a problem or a controversial topic. Students in small groups discuss the problem and try to come up with appropriate solutions. In more advanced classes, students could choose their own topic and lead a discussion about it. This activity advances turn-taking elements to topic control among the students, and reinforces accuracy of grammar and pronunciation.

Another activity is *interviewing* wherein ELLs interview a native speaker about some meaningful or memorable experience in their lives. After the interview, the students organize the information collected and present it to the whole class.

Observation Activities

These are activities in which students record both verbal and nonverbal interactions between native speakers or advanced speakers of the target language. This process helps students become aware of the language spoken in an authentic setting. It also allows students to observe how people greet each other, make requests, interrupt each other, compliment each other, disagree, or receive compliments. A follow-up activity could be a role play created by the students to show the verbal and nonverbal behaviors appropriate in a particular situation.

Discussion Activities

- **Describing pictures:** Each group has a picture that all members of the group can see. The secretary makes a check mark for each sentence (the secretary does not have to write out the sentence) the members of the group use to describe the picture. After two minutes, the check marks are added up, and the group tries to surpass their checks by describing a second picture.
- **Picture differences:** Each pair is given a set of two pictures. Without showing their picture to their partner, they must find out what differences there are between the pictures by questioning each other.
- **Solving a problem:** Students are told that they will be on an educational advisory committee that has to advise the principal on a problem with students. They should discuss their recommendations and write a letter to the principal. (Teacher needs to prepare the problem and copy it for each student or group.)

Performance Activities

In performance activities, language learners prepare for the activity beforehand and deliver a message to a group. This could vary from a student's speech or explanation of an experiment to simply telling a story from their own experience. The follow-up activity could involve videotaping the students during their performances and having them evaluate themselves. This allows the students to focus on communication about their initial performance and, in the follow-up session, deal with specific language features. Additionally, role play and dramas can be used for all language learners, making varying demands on the learners according to their proficiency levels. Finally, debates can be an effective performance activity for intermediate and advanced learners.

- **Creative drama:** This activity can be used in the language classroom to encourage dialogue technique. Students either write their own play or learn one from English literature. The activity is time consuming, but increases confidence and morale of the ELLs.
- **Role plays and skits:** ELLs are each given a card describing their situation and the task or problem. The participants can be given time to practice their role play or they may improvise. This activity is usually done in pairs or small groups. (Adapted from Ur, 1996)

These activities and tasks can be adjusted to the levels and needs of the ELLs.

An ESOL instructor can use a variety of instructional methods to communicate with students. Common techniques which are suitable for all levels are:

Contextual
- Gestures
- Body language
- Facial expressions
- Props
- Visual illustrations
- Manipulatives

Linguistic Modifications
- Standardized vocabulary
- Set standard for sentence length and complexity
- Reinforcement through repetition, summarization, and restatement
- Slower speaking pace

Teaching Vocabulary
- Use of *charades* when trying to communicate a word (acting out the word with physical actions or gestures)
- Introducing new vocabulary through familiar vocabulary
- Utilizing visual props, antonyms, and synonyms to communicate vocabulary

As English Language Learners progress, these techniques are adjusted according to individual or group needs and proficiency levels.

Skill 6.2	Knowledge of formal and informal methods of assessing oral language proficiency

Everything a teacher does to check on student learning in the classroom is a type of informal (also called formative) assessment. This includes comprehension check activities such as thumbs up/thumbs down, verbal responses (ranging from yes/no and one or two word answers to complete sentences), end-of-lesson feedback surveys, quizzes, to name a few. The interview technique is especially effective for obtaining feedback regarding a student's developing oral language proficiency.

Teachers can use oral interviews, or paired student-to-student interviews, to evaluate the language the students are using or their ability to provide content information when asked questions—both of which have implications for further instructional planning. This type of assessment allows instructors to evaluate the student's level of English proficiency, as well as identify potential problem areas which may require correctional strategies.

Formal assessments (also called summative assessments) are usually conducted at the end of a unit of study, to check students' global learning of the content. These include national or state assessments, as well as chapter, unit or other classroom tests. At the national and state levels there are a few formal oral assessment instruments designed to test a student's overall achievement of oral language proficiency. These include, but are not limited to, the ACTFL Oral Proficiency Interview (OPI), Test of Spoken English (TSE) and, in Massachusetts, the Department of Secondary and Elementary Education (DESE)-mandated Massachusetts English Language Assessment – Oral, or MELA-O.

ACTFL Oral Proficiency Interview (OPI)
This assessment was originally created by the American Council on the Teaching of Foreign Languages (ACTFL) in the 1950s and has been evolving ever since. It is designed to measure functional speaking ability. It is a one-on-one face-to-face or phone interview between a certified ACTFL tester and a student. The interview is a structured, interactive conversation that continuously adapts to the interests, experiences and abilities of the person being tested. The interview moves through specific communication tasks specified for each of ten proficiency levels, described in the ACTFL Proficiency Guidelines-Speaking (Revised1999). Each interview is recorded and rated by one or more certified testers. If an official OPI is required, the OPI must be conducted under the supervision of the ACTFL Testing Office. For official ratings, each OPI is blindly rated by a second certified tester and an ACTFL OPI certificate is issued when a final rating is assigned. Currently, OPI testing is available in 37different languages, English among them. (Based on information from the official ACTFL website)

Test of Spoken English (TSE)
The Test of Spoken English (TSE) has been discontinued as of March 2010. This test was developed by the Educational Testing Service (ETS) to measure the ability of non-native speakers of English to communicate orally in English. The TSE measured general oral language proficiency and was administered under timed conditions. Students were asked to respond to a variety of printed and aural (listening) stimuli. Generally, these tests were used by higher education institutions, corporations and government agencies.

Massachusetts English Language Assessment – Oral (MELA-O)
Title III of the No Child Left Behind Law (NCLB) requires that states report the performance and progress of limited English proficient (LEP) students in achieving English proficiency. In addition, Chapter 386 of the Massachusetts Acts of 2003 (known as "Question 2") requires that English language learners in Massachusetts participate in assessments of English language proficiency. The Massachusetts English Proficiency Assessment (MEPA) program was developed to comply with these federal and state requirements. The MEPA tests are based on the English Language Proficiency Benchmarks and Outcomes for English Language Learners (ELPBO). All LEP are therefore required to participate in the entire MEPA, except those who require an alternate assessment, those who require a test accommodation that is not available, and some deaf or hard of hearing students. All LEP students are required to participate in the MELA-O, except those whose Individualized Education Plans (IEPs) indicate a primary disability of deaf or hard of hearing.

In Massachusetts, teachers must be aware of the MELA-O because, at least in all public schools, it is a federal- and state-mandated assessment of all English Language Learners' oral proficiency levels (unless exempted for the reasons described in the preceding paragraph). The following is intended as a brief overview of this required assessment.

As one component of the two-part MEPA, the MELA-O assesses the proficiency of Limited English Proficient (LEP) students/ELLs in the listening (comprehension) and speaking (production) domains at grades K-12. It is an observational assessment instrument developed in the early 1990s; students are observed individually by a QMA or Qualified MELA-O Trainer (QMT) and their proficiency level is measured using the 6-point MELA-O Scoring Matrix. This rubric can be found in Appendix D of the ELPBO. The MELA-O rubric also clearly states that placement and programming decisions should be based on results of both the MELA-O and other assessments of student proficiency in the reading and writing domains. LEP students' scores on both the MEPA-R/W (Reading/Writing) and the MELA-O, therefore, are used to determine a student's overall MEPA score. Based on this overall score, the LEP student's performance can be classified as one of four levels of English proficiency: Beginning, Early Intermediate, Intermediate and Transitioning.

The MELA-O uses a 6-point scale (from 0 to 5 points) to assess each student's speaking and listening proficiency, with separate scores in the following areas:

- Comprehension
- Production, divided into four sub-domains:
  - Fluency
  - Vocabulary
  - Pronunciation
  - Grammar

Generally, both the MEPA-R/W and the MELA-O are administered each spring. However, there is also a fall assessment period for those who did not participate the previous spring. This is in order to determine a baseline performance which will be compared to the student's performance on the same assessment the following spring.

The MELA-O is administered during the administration periods set by MA DESE. It must be conducted by a Qualified MELA-O Trainer (QMT) or a Qualified MELA-O Administrator (QMA), certified by MA DESE; only QMAs and QMTs are eligible to rate ELLs. However, this does not mean that a classroom teacher must be a QMA or QMT, although s/he may be. If an educator would like to be qualified, education degree candidates should check with their institution, or, once hired, teachers should check with the MA DESE or their school to find out about additional training and certification. If a classroom teacher is not yet a QMA, the teacher should consult with the school's department head to see which staff at their school has been trained in order to ensure his/her LEP students are assessed, in compliance with the law.

The QMA or QMT administering the MELA-O will observe students primarily in classroom settings while engaging in interactive academic activities with the classroom teacher and/or classmates. Multiple observations are usually required for each student. These observations must last long enough to ensure a valid and reliable sample of the student's language proficiency. QMAs and QMTs must score only what s/he sees and hears during the observation of the student, without making assumptions about the student's communicative intentions; that is, the observer can only use the language provided during the observation period in order to determine a student's rating, even if s/he knows that the student can produce more. All MELA-O scores must be reported to MA DESE in accordance with specifications in current MEPA administration manuals.

Skill 6.3   Guidelines for selecting and administering oral language assessments

Informal assessments allow teachers to track the ongoing progress of their students regularly and often. Standardized tests measure students at a particular point of the school year (therefore, of their cumulative development by the time of administration), whereas ongoing informal assessments can provide snapshots of the continual development throughout the year. Informal assessments allow teachers to pinpoint each student's specific problem areas, plan and implement appropriate interventions (adapt their instruction). In order to continually assess a student's oral proficiency development, a teacher should use a variety of strategies and techniques. Performance-based and portfolio assessments can help a teacher document student progress in this domain.

All assessments, even informal ones, should be implemented using a scoring rubric to measure student progress. Students should be assessed at the very beginning of the school year in order to establish a baseline of their working (productive) knowledge. The first step for any teacher in the selection and administration of oral performance assessment should be to use (or create) a rubric listing outcomes outlined in the state's curriculum frameworks for their content area. For an ESL teacher in Massachusetts, these are listed in the ELPBO. Performance-based assessments typically promote a broad range of responses, rather than a single correct answer. In addition to interviews (described in Skill 6.1), other activities that can be implemented with a scoring rubric to assess students' current proficiency levels and ongoing development include:

- Reading aloud (to check for oral fluency)
- Retelling stories (to check for productive vocabulary/grammar)
- Role playing
- Giving descriptions, directions or instructions orally
- Telling a story based on visual prompts (e.g., a sequence of three or more pictures)
- Brainstorming
- Playing games
- Comprehension checks

- Exit tickets (e.g., 3-2-1: list three things you learned today, list two things you would like to know more about, list 1 thing you enjoyed/did not enjoy/did not understand at all, etc.)

With beginner/intermediate level ELLs, it is best to assess no more than three items at a time. For example, for a role-playing activity, a teacher might assess ELLs' ability to respond to "wh" questions, ask for or respond to a clarification, read addresses or telephone numbers aloud.

Informal/formative assessments should be continuous and applied on a daily, weekly, monthly continuum throughout the school year.

Formal assessment of ELLs is required by federal (NCLB) and state ("Question 2") law. In Massachusetts, this requirement is fulfilled by administering the MEPA-R/W and MELA-O. Administration periods and requirements for this formal assessment of ELLs are specified by the MA Department of Secondary and Elementary Education. In addition, unless exempted by a documented special need, all students in MCAS grades (3-12), regardless of English proficiency level, are required to participate in the MCAS.

Skill 6.4 Interpretation and use of assessment results, including differentiation between normal variation in oral language performance and performance that may indicate possible disabilities

A basic premise of assessment is "test what you teach." In the high-stakes testing of today, teachers are expected to show good results with the exit tests of their students. Teachers can use regular classroom testing to determine and monitor each individual student's strengths and weaknesses. By aligning instruction of the ELLs with the curriculum, the instructor can plan reinforcement of deficit skills as needed. This system is effective in preventing later gaps when more complex skills are introduced. By integrating language skills into the content area at all times, the instructor can make the language classroom a motivating place, with many opportunities for further learning. Instruction may be differentiated to accommodate a variety of learning styles and levels.

 Gurel (2004) claims that research evidence points to disproportionate numbers of English language learners who have been identified with learning disabilities, and at the same time, under-identification of English-language learners who have disabilities but have been dismissed because they were in the process of learning a new language. It is this conundrum that confounds the teaching of English language learners with disabilities (ELLs). Of vital importance is the accurate assessment of these students.

Assessment is diagnostic and ongoing, whereas evaluation is used to judge students' learning (Cobb, 2003 in Tompkins, G. E., 2009). Authentic assessment tools and tests give a more complete picture of what the student knows about the subject matter as well as the strategies and skills they use, whereas tests compare student performance against grade-level standards (Wilson, Martens, & Arya, 2005 in Tompkins, G. E., 2009). Oftentimes, tests are more a measure of English language proficiency than the construct which they were designed to test (Figueroa & Garcia, 1994 in Quiocho & Ulanoff, 2009). Test results may be influenced by ELLs from many different language backgrounds (Quiocho & Ulanoff, 2009).

Teachers can use the information gathered from their testing in different ways (Chapman, D. W. and Snyder, Jr., C. W. 2000):

- Tests can be used to orient and "slant" teaching practices in desirable ways.
- Teachers can be motivated to improve their teaching.
- Testing gives information for remedial work.

Creece (2003 in Schumm 2006) suggests that classroom progress be used instead of IQ-achievement discrepancy as the criteria for placing students in special education classes. In the case of students demonstrating possible learning difficulties, the classroom teacher will have preliminary diagnostics with which to recommend further testing.

Watson (2011) suggests that teachers look at the following skills when evaluating oral language skills:

Strengths
- Strong articulation skills
- Quite fluent orally
- Uses voice intonation and good expression
- Grade appropriate use of grammar
- Good use of words
- Expanding vocabulary

Weaknesses
- Weak articulation skills
- Difficulty with oral language; uses lots of interjections and hesitations (umm, uh, well...
- Weak verbal expression
- Grammar skills are quite weak
- Forgets a lot of words and can't often remember what he/she was going to say
- Weak vocabulary

Many of these oral skill weaknesses can be the result of learning a second language. Caution should be used when evaluating ELLs and descriptive evaluation is recommended by many researchers as being more beneficial. **Descriptive assessment** (Quiocho & Ulanoff, 2009) is a more holistic view by using data collected by a variety of methods (language samples, narrative analysis, and rating scales).Students are then analyzed using language proficiency, previous academic performance, and an emphasis on the use of multiple measures. In all cases, when classroom performance does not improve over a period of time, even with support from ELL teachers or support staff, consideration should be given to recommending the student for special education classes and /or support.

See Skill 10.4 for more information on students with possible learning disabilities.

COMPETENCY 7.0   UNDERSTAND THEORY, RESEARCH, AND PRACTICE RELATED TO DEVELOPING READING SKILLS AND READING COMPREHENSION IN ENGLISH AS A FIRST LANGUAGE

Skill 7.1   Research foundations and key features of significant reading theories and models

The two main traditional approaches to reading are the **bottom-up (phonics) approach** and **the top-down (a more language-based approach)**. Each approach has its proponents.

The **bottoms-up approach** is phonics instruction designed to "break the code" of reading in a systematic way. Students start by learning the sounds of letters, followed by letter-sound, and the syllables, words, sentences, etc. Reading is viewed as a linear, systematic process. Spelling and language are taught as separate subjects. This approach has its origins in ancient Greece.

The **top-down approach** advocates exposing students to a wide variety of literature and reading materials. Words are taught as individual need and are ready for them. The progressive movement led by John Dewey is associated with this approach. More recently Goodman developed a whole-language approach based on his own research, and the linguistics of Chomsky (1965). Typical characteristics of the whole-language approach are:

- Each student takes an individualized route to developing proficiency in reading
- Teachers provide mini-lessons when needed and act as facilitators
- Authentic literature and writing tasks are emphasized (as opposed to basal readers and supplementary materials)

Rumelhart (1976) and Stanovich (1980) advocate a middle ground between the two above approaches. Stanovich developed an **interactive-compensatory model** which recognizes the importance phonics as an important step in the reading process. The interactive-compensatory model:

- Suggests that students should receive early intensive instruction in phonological awareness and phonics, but with an emphasis on real reading and writing
- Teachers should have accurate data about each students' strengths and weaknesses
- Instruction should be differentiated based on each student's needs
- teachers should use research when considering what to teach and how to teach it

(Adapted from Schumm & Arguelles in Schumm, 2006)

Skill 7.2   The role of oral language in early reading development and the interrelationship of listening, speaking, reading, and writing

Some state policies or districts fail to recognize the importance of L1 literacy and its importance in L2 learning. (Avalos in Schumm, 2006). Cummins (1981) formulated an **interdependency hypothesis** which explains that the degree of knowledge and processes evident in the L1 will determine the ease of transfer to the L2. Many other studies since Cummins' study support this claim in the area of L2 reading (Schumm, 2006). In other words, ELLs need to develop oral language in order to develop reading skills which in turn further develop oral language skills.

Phonological awareness is a significant part of literacy development in children. Likewise, recent research has shown that phonological awareness also plays an important role as children with limited English language proficiency learn to read both in their native language (L1) and in their second language (L2). Students need to understand the words in order to read texts. To read words, they need to be aware of the letters and the sounds represented by letters. This basic learning leads to the blending of sounds that helps them to pronounce words. Reading educators have found that phonological awareness is critical to the development of comprehension skills.

Furthermore, when fluency in word recognition is achieved, the child focuses more on understanding what is read. Therefore, researchers emphasize the importance of word recognition instruction to enhance fluency. It is recommended that educators who want to improve students' comprehension skills first teach them how to decode well. Explicit instruction in sounding out words is a start in developing good comprehension skills. Word recognition skills must be developed to the point of fluency if comprehension is to be increased.

Recent research has shown that phonological awareness in the native language (L1) of the English language learners predicts successful literacy acquisition of both L1 and L2. Therefore, the closer the phonologies of L1 and L2, the more likely it is that the transfer of skills will help the English language learners in their literacy development of L2. Studies suggest beginning instruction for bilingual children with the sounds and patterns that the two languages share. Teachers can then move on to the sounds and patterns that are different between the two languages. In this way, teachers can build upon the transfer of the common sounds of both languages in order to help their students achieve literacy skills.

Instruction could follow with discussion of the sounds that are different between the two languages, to avoid negative transfer. In short, phonological awareness of both the native language and the target language can help increase the literacy skills of an English language learner. This awareness fosters not only their word recognition skills and their fluency, but also helps students focus their cognitive capabilities on increasing their reading comprehension.

Integration of all four language skills is beneficial for all English Language Learners, regardless of their proficiency level (Genesee et. al., 2006). Integration of the skills provides a framework for learners to exercise their writing skills. The integration of the four skills provides an effective context for writing so that the use of one leads naturally to the use of another, as in real life. In this way, learners will see how writing relates to certain communicative needs just as the other skills do. For example, students need to participate in classroom conversations by articulating their opinions, sharing their observations, making comparisons, etc, through speaking and writing. They need to listen to the topic, take notes, discuss with their classmates, and read about the topic, which requires the integration of all four skills.

Oral language development and language skills such as reading, writing, speaking, and listening need to be developed in conjunction with one another. They are all interrelated and integrated naturally.

- **Practice** in any one area promotes development in the other areas as well.
- **Connections** between abstract and concrete concepts are best made when all language processes are incorporated and integrated during practice and application.

English language learners benefit from opportunities to use English in multiple settings. Learning is more effective when students have an opportunity to participate fully, actively discussing ideas and information. Through meaningful interaction, students can practice speaking and making themselves understood by asking and answering questions, negotiating meaning, clarifying ideas, and other techniques. These activities require the use of the four language skills (reading, writing, speaking, and listening) in order to successfully complete each task.

Opportunities for Interaction

- Effective teachers strive to provide a more balanced linguistic exchange between themselves and their students.
- Interaction accesses the thought processes of another and solidifies one's own thinking.
- Talking with others, either in pairs or in small groups, allows for oral rehearsal of learning.

It is important to encourage students to elaborate on their verbal responses and challenge them to go beyond "yes" and "no" answers:

- "Tell me more about that."
- "What do you mean by. . .?"
- "What else. . .?"
- "How do you know?"

It is also important to allow wait time for students to formulate answers. If necessary, the teacher can also call on another student to extend his or her classmate's response.

All students, including English language learners, benefit from instruction that frequently includes a variety of grouping configurations. It is recommended that at least two different grouping structures be used during a lesson:

- **Flexible small groups**
  - To promote multiple perspectives
  - To encourage collaboration

- **Partnering**
  - To provide practice opportunities
  - To scaffold instruction
  - To give assistance before independent practice

Additionally, teachers should provide activities that allow interaction with varied student groupings.

- Group students homogeneously by language proficiency, language background, and/or ability levels.
- Heterogeneous variety maintains students' interest.
- Movement from whole class, to partners, to small group increases student involvement.
- Heterogeneous grouping can challenge students to a higher level and provide good student models.
- Varying group structures increases the preferred mode of instruction for students.

Cooperative Learning Ideas

- **Information gap activities:** Each student in a group has only one or two pieces of the information needed to solve the puzzle or problem. Students must work together, sharing information, while practicing their language and using critical thinking skills.
- **Jigsaw:** Jigsaw a reading task by chunking text into manageable parts (1–2 pages); students pool their information.
- **Roundtable:** Use with open-ended questions, grammar practice. Small groups of students sit at tables, with one sheet of paper and a pencil. A question, concept, or problem is given to each group by the teacher; students pass paper around table, each writing his or her own response. Teacher circulates room.
- **3-Step Interview:** Students are paired. Each student listens to the other as they respond to a topic question. At the end of three minutes, each pair joins

another pair of students and shares what their partners said. This activity provides students with a good way to practice language.

- **Writing Headlines:** This activity provides a way to practice summarizing an activity, story, or project. Teacher provides models of newspaper or magazine headlines. Students work in pairs writing a headline for an activity. Pairs share their headlines with the rest of the class and the class votes on the most effective headlines.

Wait Time

Wait time varies by culture. Research has shown that the average amount of wait time in American classrooms is not sufficient. Teachers should

- Allow students to express their thoughts fully without interruption.
- Allow students to discuss their answer with a partner before sharing with the whole group.

Fluency is developed over time through extensive practice both in speaking and in reading. Ample opportunities should be given to ELLs to develop their speaking and listening abilities to help them achieve more oral fluency. Role plays, skits, poems, singing, and telephone dialogs are good ways to increase oral fluency. Fluency in reading interacts with oral fluency. Wide exposure to print and reading will increase both reading fluency and oral fluency. The two are intertwined.

Fluent readers are able to grasp chunks of language, read for meaning (and not word by word), and decode automatically. They are confident readers who are able to self-monitor, and maintain comprehension. Specific instruction devoted to these areas should improve fluency rates in slower readers.

Second-language teaching (SLT) recognizes the importance of giving ELLs integrative tasks which further their language goals by including any or all of the following language skills: listening, speaking, reading, writing, and viewing. Tasks are loosely defined as any activity which emphasizes meaning over form. Which tasks are chosen depends on the teacher who makes decisions about appropriate tasks for her classroom.

Literacy is a complex set of skills that comprise the interrelated processes of reading and writing. Reading requires decoding, accurate and fluent word recognition, and comprehension at the word, phrase, sentence, and text levels. Writing requires automatic letter formation and/or keyboarding, accurate and fluent spelling, sentence construction, and the ability to compose a variety of different text structures with coherence and cohesion.

Literacy involves the integration of speaking, listening, and critical thinking. Young children use their oral language skills to learn to read, while older children use their reading ability to further their language learning. The instructional components necessary for reading and writing include: phonemic awareness, phonics, vocabulary building, fluency development, comprehension, text structure, and writing process strategies, as well as prerequisite writing skills, such as handwriting, spelling, and grammar.

A survey of research points to the following indicators of effective instructional literacy practices:

- Motivating students according to their unique needs and interests
- Providing direct explicit instruction of reading and writing skills and strategies based on ongoing student assessment
- Modeling the effective thinking skills that good readers and writers employ
- Devoting fifty percent of the students' instructional time on a daily basis to reading and writing in the classroom
- Activating students' prior knowledge to help them make connections between what they know and what they would like to learn (e.g., KWL)
- Providing opportunities for students to make text and writing connections to their lives, forms of media, and the world
- Offering both guided and independent reading experiences
- Differentiating instruction with a plentiful supply of multi-level books to accommodate interests and ability levels
- Motivating readers by offering a choice of books to read that are at their independent reading level, and that they can read with accuracy, fluency and comprehension
- Promoting conversation through purposeful and guided discussion about a book, piece of writing, or topic
- Guiding discussions through open-ended questioning
- Creating a more personable learning environment
- Designing projects that excite and engage students as opposed to engaging in short disconnected tasks (integration of subjects)
- Assessing student work based on common rubrics

Skill 7.3   Knowledge of the alphabetic principle, and research-based strategies for promoting students' phonemic awareness and other critical phonological skills (e.g., phonics skills)

The International Reading Association (1997) issued a position statement on the place of phonics in reading instruction. This position paper asserts that phonics has an important place in beginning reading instruction, primary teachers value and teach phonics, and effective phonics is integrated into the total language arts program. To help children learn phonics, teaching analytical phonics in context seems to work better than teaching synthetic phonics in isolation, e.g. on worksheets.

Some of the techniques for beginning reading development, skills and strategies are glossed below:

- Teaching children to understand sentences, texts, and other materials is better than trying to teach the word skills in isolation.
- Children can learn the alphabet principles by alphabetizing lists of spelling words or groups of objects.
- Simple techniques such as holding up the left hand and recognizing the letter 'L' can help children remember which side of the text to begin reading first.
- Learning to decode words is best achieved by practicing while reading.
- Sight words can be memorized.
- Three major types of context clues are: syntactic (word order, word endings, function of words in a sentence), semantic (meaning clues), and phonemes and graphemes (/ph/ may sound like /f/ as in photograph, /ch/ sometimes sounds like a /k/ as in chemistry).
- Reading fluency may be improved by observing the following strategies (et al): reread for clarity and to improve understanding, ask for help when confused, realize that "There is no such thing as a stupid question". Venn diagrams, webs, and other graphics may be helpful in organizing texts for easier understanding.
- Vocabulary cards or dictionaries may help ELLs to recall words they don't know. Word walls and instruction on idioms, antonyms, synonyms, and homonyms are useful.
- Learning the structure of sentence patterns, question forms, and their punctuation can help the ELL to determine meaning.

Teaching decoding skills is considered to be one of the effective methods of reading instruction. The emphasis is on teaching the phoneme-grapheme correspondences. In order to develop effective reading skills, students should aim for *automaticity* i.e., the brain process of decoding letter sounds becomes automatic. Automaticity leads to fluent reading whereby the brain may process many letters, sounds, and words at the same time, which is positively related to students' achievement in reading. Once decoding skills are mastered, more attention can be given to mastering the overall meaning of a phrase or sentence (comprehension). However, students still need explicit instruction in developing strategies to improve their comprehension skills.

Phonics and other linguistic approaches to teaching reading are important in terms of word identification skills. Accurate and rapid word recognition leads to fluency in reading, which is considered one of the five critical components of the reading process (National Reading Panel). When the reader's decoding skills become automatic, she or he is able to focus attention on constructing meaning. For readers who have not yet reached automaticity of decoding skills, reading is a slow, laborious, struggle. Fluent readers are more likely to engage in extensive reading than struggling readers. The view that if readers read more, they will achieve fluency is not applicable for ESL learners. Expert teacher guidance is necessary for learners to reach fluency. Several studies have focused on the type of instruction that would increase fluency in readers.

These instructional practices include:

- Modeled reading
- Repeated reading of familiar text
- Wide independent reading
- Coached reading of appropriately selected materials
- Chunking of text
- Word reading practice

Although fluency is an important part of reading, it is in itself not sufficient to insure high levels of reading achievement and comprehension. Fluency is based on a foundation of oral language skills, phonemic awareness, familiarity with letter forms, and efficient decoding skills. In short, a combination of instruction in decoding and reading comprehension is required for students to achieve high levels of reading skill.

Activities should be organized to encourage English language learners to use all four language skills needed to engage in real-life communicative situations. In order to do this, students should speak not only with the teacher, but also with other students. The student will also listen and try to comprehend what other speakers are saying. The listener can then react by writing down for a reader his version of the information he has just heard. This sequence of activities helps ELLs brainstorm ideas in the target language before they put them on paper, thereby providing little opportunity for the student to translate his or her idea from his or her native language into English. In this scenario, prewriting techniques give the students opportunity to use all of the four skills to help them explore and initiate their ideas on a given topic, or to develop a topic for a writing activity based on communication activities in the classroom.

Brainstorming
Brainstorming allows students working together in the classroom in small groups to say as much as they can about a topic. This helps them generate ideas to use for their individual brainstorming on paper. This activity involves the use of both speaking and listening skills to produce effective writing.

Guided Discussion
Another way to get students to talk about a topic or to focus on specific aspects of a topic is to provide guidelines for group or whole class discussion. This technique offers the advantage of helping the students beforehand with the vocabulary and sentence forms that they might need in their discussion. This again makes use of all four skills to guide students in their writing process.

Some of the other activities that encourage students to use the four linguistic skills are:

- Interviews
- Skits
- Dictation
- Note taking
- Story telling

Second-language teaching (SLT) recognizes the importance of giving ELLs integrative tasks which help them achieve their language goals by including any or all of the following language skills: listening, speaking, reading, writing, and viewing. Tasks are loosely defined as any activities which emphasize meaning over form. Which tasks are chosen depends on the teacher who makes decisions about appropriate tasks for his or her classroom.

Candlin (1987, in Batstone 1994: 17) suggests that beneficial tasks are those that

- Encourage learners to attend to meaning
- Give learners flexibility in problem solving
- Involve learners whose personality and attitude is primary
- Are challenging, but not too demanding
- Raise ELLs' awareness of the process of language use, encouraging them to reflect on their own language use

Tasks can be divided into two different types. **Learning tasks** are those that focus on formal features of language and have specific learning outcomes.

Communicative tasks are typically focused on meaning and are frequently open-ended. Often they are used in group work and may have a written component which summarizes the work.

Tasks may be divided into three main groups:

- **Information-gap tasks:** Involve the transfer of given information from one person to another, from one form to another, or from one place to another. The activity often involves selection of relevant information, as well, and learners may have to meet criteria of completeness and correctness in making the transfer.
- **Reasoning-gap tasks:** Involve deriving some new information from given information through processes of inference, deduction, practical reasoning or a perception of relationships or patterns.
- **Opinion-gap tasks:** Involve identifying and articulating a personal preference, feeling, or attitude in response to a given situation.

(Adapted from Prabhu, 1987: 46-47.)

Authenticity is an important component of tasks in the classroom. Many instructors and researchers believe that learning tasks should be authentic or use "real" spoken English. According to Nunan (1989) the distinction between real world tasks and pedagogic tasks may be blurred in reality. He believes that pedagogic activities, while they may seem artificial, may in fact practice enabling skills such as fluency, discourse, and interactional skills, mastery of phonological elements, and mastery of grammar. He suggests that there may be no hard and fast distinction between real-world and pedagogic tasks.

Skill 7.4   Knowledge of research-based strategies to help students determine the meaning of unfamiliar words in text, expand their reading vocabulary, develop their reading comprehension, and address different types of reading materials and purposes for reading

During efficient reading, incoming textual data is processed (bottom-up), which activates appropriate higher level schemata (top-down) against which the reader tries to give the text a coherent interpretation. The reader makes predictions on the basis of these top-down processes and then searches the text for confirmation or rejection of these partially satisfied higher-order schemata.

Many people wait for a reading passage to present the information in an organized way for them. However, **reading comprehension** is a highly complex area where successful readers use reading strategies in each of the three distinct phases of reading—prereading, reading, and postreading—to successfully understand a text (Peregoy and Boyle, 2008).

- The purposes of the "prereading reading phase" are for teachers to build background knowledge through anticipation guides or field trips, motivate the reader with structured overviews or films, and establish the purpose using experiments or pictures.
- The purposes of the "reading phase" are to read, based upon the established purpose, using learning logs or annotating texts to record information, improve comprehension by Directed Reading-Thinking Activities and asking questions, and utilizing background knowledge by studying headings and subheadings and answering questions.
- The purposes of the "postreading phase" are to help the student with organizing and remembering information through activities such as art work, maps, or summaries and to use the information in reporting, making a film, or publishing.

Some of the techniques students need to be able to master in reading comprehension include:

- Skimming to extract main idea
- Scanning for specific information
- Predicting based upon prior knowledge
- Restating the information to indicate comprehension of the text
- Recognizing inferred information
- Sounding out unfamiliar words, guessing at their meaning based upon previous understanding of the text
- Summarizing the text.

Teachers can guide students through these steps by using scaffolding techniques and giving support as needed.

Children's and juvenile's literature includes parables, fables, fairy tales, folktales, myths, legends, novels, romances, poetry, drama, and novels. ELLs need to be taught the intricacies of plot, point of view, setting, characterization, and other literary terms just as their native speaking classmates do. Many of these terms are universal, but the instructor should be aware that the literature of other cultures may vary considerably from its English counterpart. Drawing on background knowledge of ELLs is valuable, but literary genre and terms will undoubtedly have to be taught. Encouraging and promoting wide reading of the different genre both inside and outside the classroom is one way to introduce these elements to the students.

Reading classes should include instruction of the grammatical elements which typically occur over large stretches of text. Authentic texts contain more complex grammatical constructions, like anaphoric reference and cohesive devices, which result in second-language readers having difficulty synthesizing information across sentences and paragraphs. Additionally, vocabulary building is an important aspect of reading instruction in order to avoid breakdown in the process of reading. The teacher can help students read a passage by preparing them with a brief list of some of the most important terms, together with their meanings in the context before they read. However, only those words should be pretaught which are important in order to read the text accurately and critically.

The cultural dimension to reading involves one's purposes for reading and the attitude one holds towards the book and its content. Therefore, the teacher needs to utilize techniques and instructional practices which take attitudes based on cultural background of learners into account. One effective technique is to give students ample opportunities to work in pairs and small groups in which they share with each other the process of reading and literacy in their own cultures.

COMPETENCY 8.0 **UNDERSTAND READING INSTRUCTION AND ASSESSMENT FOR ENGLISH LANGUAGE LEARNERS**

Skill 8.1 **Differences in initial reading instruction in English for students who are and are not literate in their first language**

Children learn to read only once. If they are able to read in their native language, they are able to read in English. It is important for ELLs to increase their vocabulary and knowledge of the structure of English, their second language. By building on what the ELL already knows with regard to literacy, language, and experiences in his or her native language, teachers will be able to improve the reading level of the ELL in English. For this reason, it is necessary to evaluate the ELL in his or her first, native, or heritage language in order to initiate the best reading instruction in English.

For these transitional readers, explanations in the L1 will be beneficial because they will be able to compare and contrast new information with information about their L1.

Sometimes ELLs entering the U.S. school system have not had schooling in their L1 or the opportunity to learn to read in the L1. In this case, it may be necessary to begin reading instruction in English. These students will not have the benefit of academic instruction in reading and will need to begin reading instruction similar to that of beginning native speakers. However, teachers should bear in mind that their native language may or may not contain linguistic features that are similar to the English language. Dulay, Burt, & Krashen (1982 in Quiocho & Ulanoff, 2009) state that a knowledge of how young native speakers construct the rules and structure of English will benefit teachers more in understanding ELLs' difficulties with the language than contrastive linguistics.

Teaching initial literacy should focus on concepts about print (Clay, 1983 in Quiocho & Ulanoff, 2009), phonemic awareness, and phonics (Challl, 1983 in Quiocho & Ulanoff, 2009). Zainuddin et al (2007) claims that ELLs who come from different backgrounds and varying literacy experiences may benefit from instruction that emphasizes skill building at the word and sentence levels as well as comprehension of different types of reading materials. Texts, such as, predictable stories, poems, public signs, advertisement clips, and songs are all helpful in exploring the purpose and nature of reading.

Skill 8.2 **The relationship and transfer of existing first-language reading skills to the second language and factors that affect second-language reading development**

Literacy development is affected not only by the individual students' educational background but also by the educational background of their families. With respect to individual ESOL students, it is paramount to note that some adolescent ELLs need to learn to read for the first time, while others are building second or third language literacy with already developed first language literacy (Peregoy & Boyle, 2000). Therefore, those students who lack literacy skills in their first language have inadequate skills to succeed in school and need basic as well as advanced literacy development.

Literacy requires a number of cognitive and metacognitive skills that students can transfer from their first language to their second or third language. In addition, students literate in their first language have more funds of knowledge or prior knowledge to comprehend the content of the text. The educational background of the ELLs gives them the advantage of transferring their first language literacy skills to their second language and using their prior literacy knowledge to understand the new information. With respect to writing, research has shown that students who lacked first language literacy strategies displayed a similar lack of strategies for writing in their second language. Mohan and Lo (1985) suggest that students who have not developed good strategies in their first language would not have developed strategies to transfer to their second language. Similarly, transfer of knowledge from L1 literacy helps students brainstorm information to help them write about the topic at hand.

Furthermore, family literacy of the English language learners also has an impact on their literacy development. The educational level of the parents has a great influence on literacy development, reflecting the family's attitude towards education and the value they give to success in school. Parents with positive attitudes towards education are more involved in school activities and keep track of their child's progress. They attend parent-teacher conferences and are a part of the learning process. In addition, parents who read books to children from an early age and have books, newspapers, magazines and other reading materials available at home, facilitate their children's literacy development. These families spend time reading together and encourage critical thinking and high-order skills in their children. These positive attributes help students develop skills that are critical for success in school.

Research suggests that, contrary to many popular myths, immigrant families, poor families, and other minority group families do value literacy and education. Although literacy varies in different families, literacy serves many functions in families living below the poverty level, families in which English is not the primary language, and families with low educational levels (Peregoy and Boyle, 2008). Teachers need to be perceptive and draw upon the child's home language and literacy experiences so that the child is better served when beginning literacy instruction.

Encouraging home involvement in the literacy process is critical. Family members are modeling reading and writing every time they read the newspaper or magazine, make a shopping list, note an appointment on a calendar, discuss their work schedule, or question the newest charges on the phone bill. Many children come from societies where oral storytelling traditions (e.g., Navajo, Spanish, Hmong, or African-American) provide excellent foundations for literacy development.

Nevertheless, little research has been conducted about how to teach ELLs with limited literacy in their first language—whether a young child or an older one. If feasible, students should first learn to read in their native language and later in the second language. When instruction is begun in English, many ESOL practitioners believe that the same methods used to teach the native speaker will be beneficial to the ELL because similar literacy patterns will probably emerge. Older learners may be able to progress more rapidly because they use their worldly experiences to help them with comprehension and communication.

National reading authorities recommend phonemic awareness, phonics, reading fluency, and comprehension as the keys to success in achieving literacy. All of these elements should be considered in meaningful contexts rather than in isolation. Instruction in specific strategies (e.g., summarizing, retelling, and answering questions) will help the ELLs to become independent readers and writers.

Teachers can also use the similarities and differences of the different languages to teach learning strategies. For example, the adjective comes before the noun in English but in Spanish it comes after the noun. A text written in English is expected to have a main idea and several supporting details to explain or support it. Other languages are more descriptive and depend on the beauty of the language to convey the writer's meaning. By using the concept of cognates, both true and false, teachers can improve vocabulary development.

Schumm (2006) emphasizes that not only are the reading level characteristics important, but also the differences between L1 and L2, because these may influence the assumed level of the student. Some of the questions she proposes to elicit these similarities and differences are for further evaluation of reading level characteristics:

- Is the L1 writing system logographic like Arabic, syllabic like Cherokee, or alphabetic like English and Greek?
- How does the L1 syntax compare with the L2 syntax?
- Are the spelling patterns phonetic with consistent grapheme-phoneme relationships (e.g., Spanish or French) or are there multiple vowel sounds (e.g., English)?
- Do students read from left to right and top to bottom in their L1?
- Are there true cognates (Spanish, *instrucción* and English, instruction) and false cognates (Spanish, *librería* <bookstore> and English, library) that will help or confuse the ELL?
- Are the discourse patterns and writing styles of L1 and L2 similar or different?
- Are questions with known answers asked (teacher questions) or are rhetorical questions (found among many working class families) asked?
- Is L1 writing style circular, with long sentences and many details (e.g., Spanish) or linear, with the minimum number of facts or supporting details needed to support the main idea (e.g., English)?

Additionally, recent research has shown that, for English language learners, phonological awareness in the native language (L1) predicts successful literacy acquisition in both L1 and a second language (L2). In other words, phonological awareness skills developed in L1 transfer to L2 and facilitate L2 literacy development. Phonological awareness skills are known to develop in a predictable pattern, which is the same from one language to another (i.e., from larger to smaller units of sound - from word to syllable to onset-rime to phoneme). Phonological awareness skills developed in one language can transfer to another language.

Peregoy & Boyle (2008) state that literacy scaffolding helps ELLs with reading and writing at a level that would otherwise be impossible for them. Scaffolding allows ELLs to work at their level in both reading and writing, and at the same time, challenges them to reach their next level of development. To help students achieve their next level, several criteria are suggested:

- Use of functional, meaningful communication found in whole texts
- Use of language and discourse patterns that repeat themselves and are predictable
- A model (from teacher or peers) for understanding and producing particular written language patterns
- Support of students at a level Krashen refers to as *i* + 1.
- Discarding supports when the student no longer needs them.

Keeping in mind the scaffolding theory, teachers may use the first language in instruction—when they know it. This is not always possible. In many states, there are hundreds of language communities represented in the statewide school system. A danger of this method is that some students become dependent on instruction in their first language and are reluctant to utilize their knowledge of the second language. However, for most children, instruction in their first language has numerous advantages. First, language instruction lowers the affective filter by reducing tension, anxiety, and even fear, thus permitting faster learning; it can clarify misunderstandings in the second language content; and it can be used to explain how the two languages differ or are the same with respect to different types of reading texts or writing tasks.

Skill 8.3   Selection and adaptation of reading instruction materials for English language learners at different ages, stages of reading development, and levels of English language proficiency

Vocabulary

Research has shown that the same 1000 words (approximately) make up 84 percent of the words used in conversation and 74 percent of the words in academic texts (*The Nation*, 2001). The second most frequently used 1000 words increases the percentages to 90 percent of the words used in conversation and 78 percent used in academic texts. The ELL needs to understand 95 percent to achieve comprehension of the academic text. ELLs need to acquire the 2000 most used words and work on academic content words at the same time. In order to help students acquire the vocabulary they need for school, consider the following.

- Vocabulary development for young children is increased using the same methods used with native speaker beginning readers: ample exposure to print, word walls, realia, signs on objects around the room, and so on.
- Older children may take advantage of all these methods in addition to studying true and false cognates, creating personal dictionaries, journal writing between themselves and their teacher, and using learning strategies to augment their vocabulary.
- Other strategies, from Peregoy and Boyle (2008) are:
  - Activate the prior knowledge of the ELL.
  - Repeat the new word in meaningful contexts.
  - Explore the word in depth through demonstrations, direct experience, concrete examples, and applications to real life.
  - Have students explain concepts and ideas in writing and speaking using the new words.
  - Provide explicit strategy instruction so that students can independently understand and use the new words.

Skill 8.4   Knowledge of sheltered strategies and various reading intervention approaches for addressing the specific reading needs of English language learners

When planning pre-reading and intermediate reading intervention, the teacher may use the following intervention strategies:

WORD ANALYSIS
(e.g., concepts about print; phonemic and morphemic awareness; vocabulary and concept development; decoding; word recognition, including structural analysis, recognition of cognates, and other word identification strategies)

Sound-symbol correspondence is more difficult in English than some languages because each letter can make a variety of sounds. Recognition of repeating patterns helps students develop decoding skills. Consonant blends such as /ch/, /ph/ and /sh/ are readily recognizable and make the same sound with consistency. Earliest beginners can scan for those language patterns and recognize the sounds they make.

Recognition of **cognates** and false cognates is very helpful in decoding and can be directly taught. Many words are identical in both languages, with the only difference being pronunciation. Fortunately for students, as they develop skills in content areas such as math and science, the incidence of these cognates increases. Some examples of English-Spanish cognates are:

- Hotel
- Radio
- Religion
- Eclipse
- Editor

Many words are the same in English and Spanish, with the addition of a changed **vowel at the end of the word**. Here are some examples:

- Cost: costo
- Cause: causa
- Minute: minute
- Medicine: medicina
- List: lista
- Map: mapa

Here are some of the common **false cognates** between English and Spanish:

- Libreria – It's not a library, but a bookstore.
- Embarazada – It doesn't mean embarrassed, but pregnant.
- Asistir – It doesn't mean to assist, but to attend or be present.

Prefixes and suffixes can be directly taught to give the student scaffolding in decoding new words. For instance, -ful and –less can be taught and then combined with known words to make new ones.

- Help + ful =　helpful
- Help + less = helpless
- Care + ful =　careful
- Care + less = careless

FLUENCY

(e.g., reading aloud with appropriate pacing, intonation, and expression; applying word recognition skills)

The teacher may utilize a variety of strategies to increase fluency, such as the following:

- Duet reading, where the student reads aloud simultaneously with the teacher helps the student develop proper intonation and pacing.
- Listen/repeat exercises, including short dialogues between teacher and student or student and student.
- Choral reading, where the entire class reads aloud together, starting and stopping and emphasizing at the same points

- Singing, or language that is sung, is difficult to forget. Simple common expressions set to familiar tunes such as "Happy birthday," or "Are You Sleeping?" can be quickly invented and help develop fluency.

SYSTEMATIC VOCABULARY DEVELOPMENT
(e.g., applying word recognition skills, using content-related vocabulary, recognizing multiple-meaning words, applying knowledge of text connectors, recognizing common abbreviations, and using a dictionary, using morphemes and context to understand unknown words)

The teacher understands that second language acquisition is a jigsaw process, in which a student acquires comprehension of a word, a phrase, or a concept in ways that may seem random and unmanageable. The imposition of systematic vocabulary development, whether content-related or grouping by phonics or grammatical structures, relieves anxiety and lowers the affective filter.

- Armed with recognizable text connectors (and, but, because, until, unless, etc.), a student has a method to help break down text into manageable segments.
- Use of the dictionary, with its many abbreviations (*v.t., n.,* pronunciation symbols, etc.) empowers the student to research new words with confidence.
- Recognizing common morphemes such as the prefix *un-* can help decode un-familiar and un-known words (without becoming un-happy).

READING COMPREHENSION
(e.g., features, structures, and rhetorical devices of different types of texts; comprehension and analysis of grade-level-appropriate texts; identifying fact and opinion; identifying cause and effect; using a text to draw conclusions and make inferences; describing relationships between a text and one's own experience; evaluating an author's credibility)

The teacher can use a variety of scaffolding techniques to help students recognize features of different types of texts. For instance,

- Students can be taught key words to help differentiate fact from opinion (I believe; it seems to me…).
- Students can draw arrows between listed events from the text to determine what was a cause and what was an effect.
- Students can be directly taught to make inferences (The old woman was crying. What does that tell us?).
- Students can make text-to-self connections (Have you ever_____?).
- Students can evaluate credibility (Is the wolf a reliable narrator? Why or why not?).

LITERARY RESPONSE AND ANALYSIS
(e.g., narrative analysis of grade-level-appropriate texts, structural features of literature, literary criticism)

There are many levels of literary response and analysis the teacher can provide for even beginning ELs to use. Students can develop their own rating systems for books and movies, breaking down the text into elements that they wish to evaluate: setting, plot, characters, etc. and then applying a five-star or ten-star system to arrive at an overall evaluation.

- Students can illustrate a story to demonstrate interpretive or reflective response to it.
- Students can compare book and movie versions of the same story. Students can develop their own versions of the same story with graphic art or poetry.
- Students can use graphics to retell a story. Graphics force the student to decide which story elements are important enough to include in the blank cartoon panels provided.

The key elements of sheltered instruction are the following:

ACCESS ENGLISH LEARNERS' PRIOR KNOWLEDGE
(e.g., concepts, vocabulary related to a lesson, including using an additive cultural approach)

Schemata need to be activated to draw upon the previous knowledge and learning of the ELL, especially when the ELL may not have had experiences similar to the mainstream culture. The use of graphics to encourage pre-reading thought about a topic (e.g., brainstorming, web maps, and organizational charts) activates this knowledge and shows how information is organized in the students' minds. Shumm (2006) states that research has shown:

- More prior knowledge permits a reader to understand and remember more of new materials (Brown, Bransford, Ferrara, & Campione, 1983).
- Prior knowledge must be activated to improve comprehension (Bransford & Johnson, 1972).
- Failure to activate prior knowledge is one cause of poor readers (Paris & Lindauer, 1976).
- Good readers accept new information if they are convinced by an author's arguments. Likewise, they may reject ideas when they conflict with a reader's prior knowledge (Pressley, 2000).

CONTEXTUALIZE A LESSON'S KEY CONCEPTS AND LANGUAGE
(e.g., using materials, resources, and activities to support contextualization)

Teacher need to analyze the lesson's key concepts and then contextualize them in a way so that all students understand what the lesson is about. In a lesson on butterflies, for example, the teacher can bring in butterflies (or simply a caterpillar that is ready to change into a chrysalis) at different stages of development. Different resources such as realia, posters, books, and films can be used as resource materials for initiating instruction and activating background knowledge. All of these resources as well as classroom observations can be then used in different learning experiments, projects and writing activities.

MODIFY AND AUGMENT STATE-ADOPTED CONTENT-AREA TEXTBOOK(S) TO ADDRESS ENGLISH LEARNERS' LANGUAGE NEEDS, INCLUDING THE INCORPORATION OF PRIMARY-LANGUAGE RESOURCES

Scaffolding ELL's language needs starts with a careful analysis of the state-standards for the grade level. Differentiated instruction is permitted when the ELL does not have grade-level proficiency in the language. Planning of instruction should answer the questions of: **What** content will be taught, **Who** the student is (language and cultural background of the student), **How** (strategies and materials), and **How well** (performance goals and assessment methods). When available, resource materials in a student's first language are an acceptable scaffolding technique.

DEMONSTRATE OR MODEL LEARNING TASKS

Instructors can bring in papers, projects, mind maps, and posters from previous classes to demonstrate what is expected in a finished project. Modeling a learning task is simply illustrating whatever point or skill is expected from the learners. In Total Physical Response, a teacher would ask students to stand up (teacher stands) or sit down (teacher sits). As instructions become more complicated, the teacher illustrates (or has a student) the expected action.

USE QUESTIONS TO PROMOTE CRITICAL-THINKING SKILLS
(e.g., analytical and interpretive questions)

Questions are one of the most frequently used instructional and scaffolding strategies. Teachers should avoid rhetorical questions as many students find them silly or purposeless. Questions which call upon students to analyze (e.g. What are the parts or features of…?, How would you classify …?, What evidence do you find …?) or interpret a topic (e.g. How would you prioritize the facts …?, Would it be better if…?, Based upon what you know, how would you explain…?) are questions which call upon higher level think skills and contribute to learning.

PROVIDE ENGLISH LEARNERS WITH EXPLICIT INSTRUCTION IN METACOGNITIVE AND COGNITIVE STRATEGIES
(e.g., debriefing, using text features, using self-evaluation and reflection)

Metacognitive Strategies
The ESOL teacher is responsible for helping students become aware of their own individual learning strategies and constantly improve those strategies and add to them.

Each student should have his/her own "tool-box" of skills for planning, managing, and evaluating the language-learning process.

- **Centering your learning:** Review a key concept or principle and link it to already existing knowledge, make a firm decision to pay attention to the general concept, ignore input that is distracting, and learn skills in the proper order.
- **Arranging and planning your learning:** The following strategies help the learner maximize the learning experience: take the time to understand how a language is learned; create optimal learning conditions, i.e., regulate noise, lighting and temperature; obtain the appropriate books, etc.; and set reasonable long-term and short-term goals.
- **Evaluate your learning:** The following strategies help learners assess their learning achievements: keep track of errors that prevent further progress and keep track of progress, e.g., reading faster now than the previous month.

Cognitive Strategies

Cognitive strategies are vital to second language acquisition; their most salient feature is the manipulation of the second language. The following are the most basic strategies: "Practicing", "Receiving and Sending Messages", "Analyzing and Reasoning", and "Creating Structure for Input and Output," which can be remembered by the acronym, "PRAC."

- **Practicing:** The following strategies promote the learner's grasp of the language: practice constant repetition, make attempts to imitate a native speaker's accent, concentrate on sounds, and practice in a realistic setting.
- **Receiving and sending messages:** These strategies help the learner quickly locate salient points and then interpret the meaning: skim through information to determine "need to know" vs. "nice to know," use available resources (print and non-print) to interpret messages.
- **Analyzing and reasoning:** Use general rules to understand the meaning and then work into specifics, and break down unfamiliar expressions into parts.
- **Creating structure for input and output:** Choose a format for taking meaningful notes, practice summarizing long passages, and use highlighters as a way to focus on main ideas or important specific details.

DEVELOP ENGLISH LEARNERS' ACADEMIC LANGUAGE
(e.g., frontloading vocabulary)

Frontloading vocabulary is a strong method of assuring reading success. When students are given explanations new vocabulary they need in upcoming reading (or content classes), they are better able to handle the academic demands placed upon them. By using examples of the word in its context, asking students to decide if the word is used correctly, and asking them to draw pictures of the word, students are actively engaged in the learning process.

PROVIDE CLEAR MODELS OF EXPECTED PERFORMANCE OUTCOMES

Using rubrics to explain what is expected is an excellent way to clarify any misconceptions students may have about the assignment. Another excellent method is to show papers or projects from previous classes.

TRANSFORM TEXT FROM ONE GENRE TO ANOTHER GENRE

Examples are: Students can be asked to take a text and create a skit out of it. Skits could be changed into a short story.

PROVIDE OPPORTUNITIES FOR ENGLISH LEARNERS TO ENGAGE IN ANALYSIS AND INTERPRETATION OF TEXT, BOTH ORAL AND WRITTEN

Students can analyze and interpret texts with graphic organizers, journals, note-taking, and summaries. For beginners, teachers can provide graphics with sample entries filled in and as the students become more familiar with them, provide fewer and fewer clues.

Oral discourse may also be analyzed. Ask students: how they felt about a dialogue, how would people in their culture respond during a similar situation, what was the main idea the speaker was making, and why do you believe or disbelieve this particular speaker?

PROVIDE ENGLISH LEARNERS WITH OPPORTUNITIES TO LEARN AND USE FORMS OF ENGLISH LANGUAGE NECESSARY TO EXPRESS CONTENT-SPECIFIC ACADEMIC LANGUAGE FUNCTIONS

(e.g., analyzing, comparing, persuading, citing evidence, making hypotheses)

ELLs need opportunities to debate, write written reports, make hypotheses, etc., but in most cases, these structures will have to be taught. Citing evidence and making hypotheses are academic skills used throughout an academic's life and need to be taught beginning with simplified reports or research papers.

Teachers need to provide models of the language activity/structure they are teaching and demonstrate it to the students. The teacher can list the specific vocabulary and rhetorical structures used on the board for illustration. These forms could be copied and distributed to the class.

PROVIDE AUTHENTIC OPPORTUNITIES FOR ENGLISH LEARNERS TO USE THE ENGLISH LANGUAGE FOR CONTENT-RELATED COMMUNICATIVE PURPOSES WITH BOTH NATIVE AND NONNATIVE SPEAKERS OF ENGLISH

ELLs need the opportunity to practice English regardless of their level. By grouping ELL students with native speakers and other nonnative speakers of English they are practicing language and the social elements of communication. Many ELLs have content knowledge but may have difficulty expressing it, whereas many native speakers may not have the content knowledge necessary to complete a task. Both students benefit when working in small groups on assigned tasks.

In addition to research projects, students will enjoy working on skits, role plays, drama, and singing. Games such as Pictionary and playing charades can be adapted to content for encouraging vocabulary learning.

ASSESS ATTAINMENT OF LESSON CONTENT USING MULTIPLE MODALITIES
(e.g., verbal, nonverbal)

For mini-assessments of lessons, the teacher can ask the students to give a "thumbs up" or "thumbs down" to questions about content. Teachers can use observation to determine if students understand and are progressing or if they did not and need help. In other ways, the teacher can ask the student to make the sound of a monkey. Draw a monkey. Move like a monkey. These techniques are useful with beginners.

For more advanced learners, verbal assessment may be more appropriate. Students can be evaluated on rubrics, written work, answering structured and unstructured questions, free recall, completing graphic illustrations of text, and word associations. Formal assessments include end of chapter tests and teacher made tests.

PROVIDE COMPREHENSIBLE AND MEANINGFUL CORRECTIVE AND POSITIVE FEEDBACK TO ENGLISH LEARNERS
Feedback is valuable only if the student understands it. Teachers can illustrate the correct response, "go over the test" providing the correct answers and illustrating the most common errors, and even using mime or translators if necessary.

Skill 8.5 **Characteristics of various types of formal and informal reading assessments and their advantages and limitations for use with English language learners**

Formal reading assessments are used for state and district accountability purposes. They usually include multiple-choice questions. Some utilize the **cloze or maze** formats where a word or words are omitted and a choice of three or four words are given to fill-in the missing content.

Examples are:

- **Test of reading comprehension:** 30-minute standardized test that can be administered by teacher or reading specialists individually or to a group of students from ages 7-17. The test has 8 sub-tests and evaluates general vocabulary, syntactic similarities, paragraph reading, and sentence sequencing. End result is a Reading Comprehension Quotient. The TORC-3 gives information about a student's strengths and weaknesses in each of the comprehension components it tests.
- **Woodcock-Johnson III Diagnostic Reading Battery:** An individually administered measure used to diagnose a student student's strengths and weaknesses for needed areas of instruction. Used with students in K-16.9.

- **Gates-MacGinitie reading tests:** Norm-referenced, group-administered *lexile score* instrument that has been scientifically researched and is effective in screening K-12 students and adults. Test identifies instructional needs and generates a *lexile score*. A lexile score is a calculation of the level of comprehension a student will have with a text. The GMRT estimates that a student will understand 75% of the lexile score, and using software, generates a list of texts based on this score.
- **Degrees of reading power:** A standardized test that uses maze (or modified cloze). Students are given passages with missing words and are required to supply missing word from a multiple-choice selection. Tests for Grades 1-12 are available. DRP scores can be matched with books of appropriate reading levels.

Informal reading assessments include:

- **Informal reading inventories (IRIs):** Graded reading passages and comprehension questions
    - may include both narrative and expository passages
    - may include narrative and expository retelling checklists
    - may incorporate prior knowledge questions for each passage
    - purposes:
        - used to gauge oral reading comprehension
        - assess silent reading comprehension
        - passages read aloud by a test administrator to test listening comprehension
- **Regular student observations:** Used to observe and evaluate student comprehension performance
- **Teacher-made and textbook assessments**

(Adapted from Medina & Pilonieta in Schumm, 2006)

Skill 8.6 **Guidelines for selecting and administering various types of reading assessments; and interpretation and use of assessment information, including differentiation between normal variation in performance and performance that may indicate possible reading or learning disabilities**

The Massachusetts Department of Education (MA DOE) tests students in the English Language each year to comply with the mandates of the No Child Left Behind Act. Section 4 of the law states: *Once English learners acquire a good working knowledge of English and are able to do regular school work in English, they shall no longer be classified as English learners and shall be transferred to English language mainstream classrooms.* Students are tested in the four language skill areas: speaking, listening, reading, and writing in both social and academic settings. Beginning in 2009, the State will report these test results using different performance levels than in previous years. Detailed information of guidance and classification of Limited English Proficiency (LEP) students is available at www.doe.mass.edu./ell/edguide/

DISABILITIES

Students with disabilities are guaranteed an education under Public Law 94-142 of 1975. A key feature of the law is the requirement of an individualized education program (IEP) for any student receiving special funds for special education. However, the classification of many ELLs or the "dumping" of ELLs in special education classes has been of concern to many educators. Those testing ELLs for placement in different classes must be certain that the tests used are both reliable and valid. Reliability can be established using multiple assessment measures, objective tests, multiple raters, and clearly specified scoring criteria (Valdez-Pierce, 2003). For a test to be valid, it must first be reliable (Goh, 2004).

 Learning disabilities refer to physical, emotional, cognitive, or social components, which severely limit what is considered to be "normal" functioning behavior. Children who fall into this category can be one or more of the following: emotionally challenged, hearing-, vision-, or speech-impaired or learning disabled.

See Skill 10.4 for more information on students with possible learning disabilities.

COMPETENCY 9.0   **UNDERSTAND WRITING INSTRUCTION AND ASSESSMENT FOR ENGLISH LANGUAGE LEARNERS**

Skill 9.1   **Knowledge of approaches, practices, and strategies used to promote English language learners' writing development and writing skills (e.g., Language Experience Approach, dialogue journals)**

Language Experience Approach is an effective method to introduce children into the art of writing. The steps in the LEA are:

- Provide an experience
- Talk about the experience
- Record the dictation
- Read the text

Sometimes, children are reluctant to 'write' their own stories later because their writing is not a "perfect" model as the teacher's was. However, this may be overcome if the teacher alternates with the children when writing the stories.

There are many ways to get students to practice writing without grading the writing: learning logs, journals, and quick-writes. Teachers can devise prompts that allow the ELLs to reflect on their learning and class discussions or explore new ideas. They may rewrite complex ideas in their own words and compare, evaluate, critique, or interpret. At the end of the period, students may quickly write what they learned during the class. ELLs can write dialog either in pairs or individually. They can try using vocabulary words from their text in comprehensible paragraphs. Another idea is to write from the perspective of another person, place or thing (Adapted from Zwiers, 2007).

On the other hand, these students may be fairly sophisticated in their manipulation of language. However, their language may value other aspects of writing that are very different from the U.S. idea of a sentence (s-v-o) or a paragraph (the topic sentence and its supporting details). In essays, the idea of developing sentences of varying lengths and structures, and connecting them through the skillful use of connectors will have to be taught through skillful modeling and examples. Supplying ample resources, such as dictionaries and lists of vocabulary conventions or connectors, will be invaluable to ELLs in upper levels.

Also, students who are learning to write need to read as much as possible of the genre that they are going to be writing about. As writing takes place in multiple genres (narrative prose, poetry, mathematical proofs, historical accounts, case studies, essays, emails, and letters), students should be exposed to each particular type of writing—its organization, the thinking behind the form, the grammar, and the correct terms used in each genre—so that they are able to replicate the appropriate phrases and syntax in their writing. As nonmainstream students will not have had as much exposure to the models as native speakers, it is necessary to point out the conventions of each genre as it is studied in the classroom.

To improve children's writing, the following activities may be used:

- **Frontloading vocabulary and language functions:** Frontloading vocabulary and language function is simply pre-teaching the vocabulary and language functions that might be unfamiliar to the students during a content lesson or reading session. The goal is to increase reading comprehension.

- **Interactive journals:** Any type of journal that requires the student to write about classroom content or comment on their feelings. Journals are a low-stakes method of keeping the teacher and the student engaged in a personal dialogue.

- **Shared reading:** In this type of reading exercise, students are given their own copy of a text to follow along in while the teacher reads to them. Unrau (2008) points out some of the benefits of shared reading:
    - demonstrates the natural rhythm and beauty of the language
    - builds bridges between texts and students lives
    - provides practice in strategies that make a text comprehensible
    - models fluent reading
    - helps students build knowledge of texts and their world

- **Learning logs:** Records of what students have learned or what they are struggling to understand. Students can be asked to summarize what they have learned from a particular text. Teachers give daily feedback of what is expected in a summary. Teachers and students can use learning logs to negotiate a text's meaning.

- **Process writing:** Unrau (2008) lists 5 stages of process writing:
    - Pre-writing: Planning by brainstorming, researching, note taking, listing, clustering, organizing
    - Drafting: Selecting a format, writing drafts, deciding on an audience
    - Revising: Review or reflect on earlier drafts by rethinking, adding, dropping, rearranging, rewriting
    - Proofreading: Prepare for publication by polishing, correcting spelling, punctuation, and grammatical problems
    - Publishing: Share with an audience by reading, displaying, anthologizing, submitting for publication

- **Graphic organizers:** Unrau (2008) enumerates graphic organizers as:
    - Clusters are also known as mind-mapping, semantic mapping, mindscaping, and webbing. A simpler and less-structured form than the formal outline.
    - Characteristics outliner: similar to a cluster but more structured. Students draw an ellipse or circle in the center and then place arrows or lines between the term and its characteristics.
    - Process organizer or Flowchart: Used to organize each step in a process
    - Cause-Effect Organizer: Causes are connected to their effect by an arrow or line

- o Problem-Solution-Evaluation Organizer: Appropriately labeled boxes are filled in with the corresponding information and connected by lines or arrows
- o Compare/Contrast Organizer: A simple Venn diagram or three columns can be used to show the similarities and differences. The overlapping circles (or center column) are used to illustrate items that are the same in each concept.
- **Prereading activities:** Those activities which prepare the student for reading (Schumm, 2006)**:**
  - o Activating or building background knowledge
  - o Making predictions
  - o Word maps
  - o Previewing
  - o Picture Walk (previewing the story using the illustrations)
  - o Going beyond the printed page (e.g. using globes, films, maps, simulation games, role playing, and field experiences)
  - o Setting the Mood

Skill 9.2   Knowledge of the writing process and its applications in developing English language learners' writing proficiency

The **writing process** needs to be taught since many students come from backgrounds where writing a text or paper is very different from the U.S. conventions. They are unfamiliar with the concept of planning the paper, doing research, organizing the material, developing a thesis statement, deciding on methods of development, drafting, revising, and editing. Rubrics can be devised that are appropriate to process writing and take into consideration both the process and the product.

Reid (1987) explains the **writing process** as steps to be followed:

Composing process
Prewriting
- Choosing a subject
- Identify you audience
- Decide on the purpose of the paper

Generating material
- Narrow the topic
- Collect ideas from personal experience, observation, interviews and/or research
- Generate details about the topic through brainstorming, clustering, outlining, listing, treeing, flow-charting
- Select the most pertinent ideas and facts for the paper

Organizing the material
- Write the main idea of the essay in thesis statement
  - o Statement of opinion and/or

- o Statement of intent
- Develop paragraphs of support for thesis statement using:
  - o Topic sentences
  - o Supporting sentences which include:
    - Facts
    - Examples
    - Physical description
    - Personal experience
- Decide on methods of development to present your ideas
  - o Process
  - o Extended definition
  - o Comparison/contrast
  - o Classification
  - o Cause/effect

Drafting
- Begin writing
- Don't worry about errors
- Reread what you have written
  - o Reflect on what you have said
  - o Reconsider your ideas
  - o Evaluate your support

Once the paper is written, the students should begin the **revision process**. If this is presented as an integral part of the writing process, students will accept it more readily.

Revision process
Focus on the audience: make the essay memorable and interesting
Focus on the Purpose: make the main idea clear and strong
Editing:
- **Coherence:**
  - o all information should directly relate to the thesis statement
  - o the information in each paragraph should relate to the topic sentence
  - o use transitions between paragraphs
  - o use paragraph hooks (repetition of words that unites paragraphs)
- **Organization**
  - o The sequence of ideas must be clear
  - o The thesis statement should be narrow enough to support the author's ideas
- **Development**
  - o Clear, credible details
  - o Use of most important information
  - o Eliminate useless details or less important information
  - o Define terms where necessary

  o Simplify information where possible

- **Mechanics:**
  o Use clear, correct, and precise vocabulary
  o Strive for varied and correct sentenced structure
  o Use some short, emphatic sentences
  o Revise grammar, especially verb tenses and subject/verb agreement
  o Spell check all work
  o Use correct punctuation

Teaching the writing process is a lengthy, cumulative effort across the curriculum and amplified over the years. The youngest children learn basic story structure, middle-graders develop paragraph writing skills, and high school students learn the intricacies of the academic essay. Many times teachers will need to give mini-lessons in the writing process as it becomes necessary in the development of a particular child's writing efforts.

Skill 9.3   Selection of purposeful writing activities appropriate for a range of ages, reading abilities, and English proficiency levels

When planning meaningful and purposeful literacy activities **teachers of very young children** may set up activities for:

- Using literacy materials in dramatic play centers
- Making posters about favorite books
- Labeling classroom items
- Writing morning messages
- Recording questions and information on charts
- Writing notes to parents
- Reading and writing letters to pen pals
- Reading and writing charts and maps

For **older ELLs**, similar non-threatening activities may be used to provide needed practice. O'Malley and Pierce (1996) recommend scaffolding techniques to reduce the language demands on ELLs by:

- **Exhibits or projects:** ELLs can be involved in presenting projects or demonstrations that illustrate the concepts or procedures being tested.
- **Visual displays:** ELLs can use graphic organizers (e.g. diagrams or semantic maps) to illustrate their understanding of vocabulary and concepts.
- **Organized lists:** ELLs can present lists of concepts or terms and demonstrate understanding by organizing or sequencing them.
- **Tables or graphs:** ELLs can complete or construct and label tables and graphs to demonstrate their understanding of how data is organized and interpreted

- **Short answers:** ELLs can give short answers or explanations that focus on the content area concepts.

ELLs need to be taught listening, speaking, reading, and writing skills in an integrated fashion which attempt to mimic real-life communicative incidents. The reading of a newspaper article may lead to an oral discussion or an oral discussion may lead to research on a topic and writing about it. Since much of the same vocabulary is being used in each of these communicative incidents, each act reinforces the other and students are able to engage in meaningful learning.

Skill 9.4   Knowledge of formal elements of written English and explicit, systematic strategies for developing students' knowledge and use of different text structures (e.g., narrative, expository, persuasive) and conventions of written Standard English (e.g., mechanics, syntax, grammar, spelling)

As ELLs develop their language skills, the **four main functions of writing** should be introduced. The types of writing may be introduced formally in class, and followed up by appropriate exercises for practice. One good way to introduce the different types of exposition is through literature.

- **Narrative:** Used to tell fictional or nonfictional stories or accounts. May relate one incident or several.
- **Descriptive:** Provides information about a person, place, or thing. Descriptive writing may be fictional (as in a story) or nonfictional (as in newspaper stories or in describing a vacation spot).
- **Expository:** Explains and clarifies ideas. Frequently found in textbooks or user manuals.
- **Persuasive:** Used to convince the reader of something.

As ELLs develop formal written English, they will need instruction in the conventions of written Standard English. This instruction is best understood as a long-term process in which the writer is engaged throughout the school years.

Mechanics
Mechanics includes spelling, punctuation, capitalization, and grammar. Teaching of mechanics is one of the goals of Language Arts instruction, and as such, is taught systematically over the course of the school years.

Syntax (See Skills 4.2 and 4.3)
Syntax is best taught in context. As ELLs develop their reading skills, they are exposed to the syntax of English. They are introduced to the grammar of English, how words are put together to form sentences, the mechanics of English, word forms, and the different kinds of sentences (simple, compound, and compound-complex).

Grammar

One way to instruct ELLs is to use their own papers for mini-lessons on relevant points. Grammar begins to have more meaning as students become more fluent in the language. Direct instruction in grammar can be achieved through formal lessons for the entire class and through mini-lessons. In mini-lessons, the teacher may wish to focus on past tense verbs. Students can then look for examples of these forms in their journals or papers and correct them for practice.

Spelling

ELLs will need instruction to progress through the five stages of spelling:

- **Emergent spelling:** Students experiment with spelling/Teacher models adult writing/Encourage ELLs to talk about their writing/Encourage ELLs to notice environmental words and letters in names
- **Letter-name spelling:** Instruction in how to form letters/Encourage listening to pronunciation of words/Post a word wall/ teach consonants, consonant digraphs, and short vowels
- **Within-word spelling:** Teach long vowel spelling rules, vowel digraphs and r-controlled vowels/develop a visual sense of whether a word looks right or not/focus on silent letters in one-syllable words/ have students sort words according to patterns/use interactive writing
- **Syllables and affixes spelling:** Teach rules of syllabication and rules for inflectional endings/teach schwa sounds and spelling patterns/teach homophones, contractions, compound words, and possessives
- **Derivational relations:** Teach root words and derivational affixes/ make word clusters using root words/sort words into roots or language of origin
  (Adapted from Tompkins: Language Arts: Patterns of Practice)

Skill 9.5	Characteristics, selection, and administration of various types of formal and informal writing assessments and interpretation and use of assessment information, including differentiation between normal variation in writing development and performance that may indicate possible disabilities

Assessment is the gathering of information in order to make decisions. In education, assessments typically focus on student performance, progress, and behavior.

PURPOSES OF ASSESSMENT

In the education of students with exceptionalities, assessment is used to make decisions about the following:

- Screening and initial identification of children who may need services
- Diagnosis of specific learning disabilities
- Selection and evaluation of teaching strategies and programs
- Determination of the child's present level of performance in academics

- Classification and program placement
- Development of goals, objectives, and evaluation for the IEP
- Eligibility for a program
- Continuation of a program
- Effectiveness of instructional programs and strategies
- Effectiveness of behavioral interventions
- Accommodations needed for mandated or classroom testing

TYPES OF ASSESSMENT

Assessment types can be categorized in a number of ways, most commonly in terms of what is being assessed, how the assessment is constructed, or how it is to be used. It is important to understand these differences so as to be able to correctly interpret assessment results.

Formal vs. Informal

This variable focuses on how the assessment is constructed or scored. **Formal assessments** are assessments such as standardized tests or textbook quizzes; objective tests that include primarily questions for which there is only one correct, easily identifiable answer. These can be commercial or teacher made assessments, given to either groups or individuals. **Informal assessments** have less objective measures, and may include anecdotes or observations that may or may not be quantified, interviews, informal questioning during a task, etc. An example might be watching a student sort objects to see what attribute is most important to the student, or questioning a student to see what he or she found confusing about a task.

Standardized Tests

Formal tests are those that are administered to either groups or individuals in a specifically prescribed manner, with strict rules to keep procedures, scoring, and interpretation of results uniform in all cases. Such tests allow comparisons to be made across populations, ages or grades or over time for a particular student. Intelligence tests and most diagnostic tests are standardized tests.

Norm Referenced vs. Criterion Referenced

This distinction is based on the standard to which the student's performance is being compared. *Norm referenced* tests establish a ranking and compare the student's performance to an established norm, usually for age or grade peers. What the student knows is of less importance than how similar the student's performance is to a specific group. *Norm* Referenced tests are, by definition, standardized. Examples include intelligence tests and many achievement tests. Norm referenced tests are often used in determining eligibility for special needs services. *Criterion Referenced* tests measure a student's knowledge of specific content, usually related to classroom instruction. The student's performance is compared to a set of criteria or a preestablished standard of information the student is expected to know. On these tests, what the student knows is more important than how he or she compares to other students. Examples include math quizzes at the end of a chapter, or some state mandated tests of specific content. Criterion referenced tests are used to determine whether a student has mastered required skills.

Group vs. Individual Assessments

This variable simply refers to the manner of presentation, whether given to a group of students or on a one to one basis. Group assessments can be formal or informal, standardized or not, criterion or norm referenced. Individual assessments can be found in all these types as well.

Authentic Assessments

Authentic assessments are designed to be as close to real life as possible so they are relevant and meaningful to the student's life. They can be formal or informal, depending upon how they are constructed. An example of an authentic test item would be calculating a 20 percent sales discount on a popular clothing item after the student has studied math percentages.

Rating Scales and Checklists

Rating scales and checklists are generally self-appraisal instruments completed by the student or observation-based instruments completed by teacher or parents. The focus is frequently on behavior or affective areas such as interest, motivation, attention or depression. These tests can be formal or informal and some can be standardized and norm referenced. Examples of norm referenced tests of this type would be ADHD rating scales or the Behavior Assessment System for Children.

Screening, Diagnosis, and Placement

Intelligence tests have historically been considered relatively good predictors of school performance. These tests are standardized and norm referenced. Examples are the *Wechsler Intelligence Scale for Children-Fourth Edition (WISC-IV)*, Stanford-Binet IV, and *Kaufman Assessment Battery for Children-Second Edition (KACB-II)*. Some intelligence tests are designed for use with groups and are used for screening and identification purposes. The individual tests are used for classification and program placement. Since intelligence is a quality that is difficult to define precisely, results of intelligence tests should not be used to discriminate or define the person's potential. In recent years intelligence testing has evolved to include measures of multiple intelligences (Gardner, 1999) and these tests can further refine placement decisions for students with special needs. In many cases a significant discrepancy between scores on different intelligences helps to identify specific learning disabilities. Such measures also help show how a disability impacts performance in different areas of the curriculum.

There are many standardized achievement and educational skills tests, including state mandated testing, that are also used by school systems to help determine eligibility and placement.

MAKING INSTRUCTIONAL DECISIONS BASED ON ASSESSMENT RESULTS

Assessment is a key to providing differentiated and appropriate instruction to all students, and this is the area in which teachers will most often use assessment. Teachers should use a variety of assessment techniques to determine the existing knowledge, skills, and needs of each student. Depending on the age of the student and the subject matter under consideration, diagnosis of readiness may be accomplished through pretest, checklists, teacher observation, or student self-report. Diagnosis serves two related purposes—to identify those students who are not ready for the new instruction and to identify for each student what prerequisite knowledge is lacking.

Student assessment is an integral part of the teaching-learning process. Identifying student, teacher, or program weaknesses is only significant if the information so obtained is used to remedy those concerns. Lesson materials and lesson delivery must be evaluated to determine relevant prerequisite skills and abilities. The teacher must be capable of determining whether a student's difficulties lie with the new information, with a lack of significant prior knowledge, or with a core learning disability that must be addressed with specialized lesson plans or accommodations. The ultimate goal of any diagnostic or assessment endeavor is improved learning. Thus, instruction is adapted to the needs of the learner based on assessment information.

USING ASSESSMENT INFORMATION TO MODIFY PLANS AND ADAPT INSTRUCTION

Assessment skills should be an integral part of teacher training. Teachers are able to use pre and post assessments of content areas to monitor student learning, analyze assessment data in terms of individualized support for students and instructional practice for teachers, and design lesson plans that have measurable outcomes and definitive learning standards. Assessment information should be used to provide performance-based criteria and academic expectations for all students in evaluating whether students have learned the expected skills and content of the subject area.

For example, in an Algebra I class, teachers can use assessment to see whether students have the prior knowledge to engage in the proposed lesson. If the teacher provides students with a preassessment on algebraic expression and ascertains whether the lesson plan should be modified to include a prealgebraic expression lesson unit to refresh student understanding of the content area, then the teacher can create, if needed, quantifiable data to support the need of additional resources to support student learning. Once the teacher has taught the unit on algebraic expression, a post assessment test can be used to test student learning, and a mastery examination can be used to test how well students understand and can apply the knowledge to the next unit of math content learning.

A teacher working with students with learning disabilities will use assessment information in additional ways. For example, if assessments show a student has extreme difficulty organizing information in the visual field, a teacher may modify a worksheet in math to present only one problem positioned in a large, squared off field, with lots of white space around it, or even set up problems to be presented one problem at a time on 4x6 inch cards, etc.

By making inferences on teaching methods and gathering clues for student performance, teachers can use assessment data to inform and have an impact on instructional practices. By analyzing the various types of assessments, teachers can gather more definitive information on projected student academic performance. Instructional strategies for teachers would provide learning targets for student behavior, cognitive thinking skills, and processing skills that can be employed to diversify student learning opportunities.

APPROPRIATE WRITING ASSESSMENTS FOR ELLS WOULD BE:

Formal Assessments

- The National Assessment of Educational Progress (NAEP) (primary trait scoring)
- Test of English as a Foreign Language (TOEFL) Writing Test (holistic scoring)
- International English Language Test System (IELTS) (analytic scoring)
- Test of English for Educational Purposes (TEEP) (analytic scoring)
- Michigan Writing Assessment (analytic scoring)
- Essays with preestablished rubrics specific to the type of assignment
- Portfolios which include several pieces of writing

Informal Classroom Assessments
For teachers concerned with assessing writing in the regular classroom, Weigle (2002) offers the following criteria:

- Evaluate out-of-class writing as well as in-class writing.
- Evaluate more than one writing sample.
- Build authenticity and interactiveness into timed writing tasks.
- Use scoring instruments (e.g. rubrics) specific to the assignment and to the instructional focus of the class. Provide useful feedback to the students.

Pros of Writing Portfolio Assessment
Assessment is:

- **Integrative:** Combines curriculum and assessment which means evaluation is developmental, continuous, comprehensive, and fairer, representing program goals and reflecting writing progress over time, genres, and different conditions
- **Valid:** Closely related to material taught and what students can do
- **Meaningful:** Students see portfolios as a record of work and progress
- **Motivating:** Presents a range of challenging writing experiences in different genres; students can see similarities and differences between assignments

- **Process-oriented:** Focuses on multi-drafting, feedback, collaboration, revision, etc.
- **Coherent:** Assignments build on each other rather than being isolated assignments
- **Flexible:** Teachers can adopt different selection criteria, evaluation methods and response practices over time, emphasizing different features of writing
- **Reflexive:** Students can evaluate their improvement and consider their weaknesses, which encourages greater responsibility and independence in writing
- **Formative:** Grading may be delayed until end of course allowing teacher to provide constructive feedback without the need for early, potentially discouraging, evaluation

Cons of Writing Portfolio Assessment

- **Logistic:** May produce considerable work for teachers
- **Design:** Grading criteria need to be understood by all teachers
- **Reliability:** Need to ensure standardized grading by all raters across genres, portfolios and courses
- **Product variation:** Problem in fairly assigning a single grade to a collection varied in genre, complexity and quality, especially if assigned by a variety of teachers in different departments
- **Task variation:** Some task may be more interesting than others and therefore, elicit better writing
- **Authenticity:** Some students may get considerable outside help or plagiarize since portfolios are compiled without close teacher supervision.

(Adapted from Hyland, 2002)

COMPETENCY 10.0   UNDERSTAND INSTRUCTION AND ASSESSMENT RELATED TO THE DEVELOPMENT OF ENGLISH LANGUAGE LEARNERS' COGNITIVE-ACADEMIC LANGUAGE PROFICIENCY AND CONTENT AREA LEARNING

Skill 10.1   Strategies for teaching subject matter in English and for developing English language learners' cognitive-academic language proficiency (e.g., providing comprehensible input, providing explicit instruction in academic language and vocabulary, integrating content and language objectives, supporting students' use of English to discuss and consider subject matter content)

It is important to implement powerful instructional strategies that actively engage students from linguistically and culturally diverse backgrounds instead of allowing them to be passive participants or observers. Krashen (1981, 1982) states that students must be instructed at a level slightly higher than their competence level, i.e. $i + 1$. He believes that for a student to learn, the input must be comprehensible.

Chamot and O'Malley (1994) stated that teachers need to be aware of their students' approaches to learning and how to expand the students' repertoire of learning strategies.

Arreaga-Mayer (1998) puts forward constructs for effective instruction to linguistically and culturally diverse students:

1. **Challenge**
   - Implicit (cognitive challenge, use of higher-order questions)
   - Explicit (high but reasonable expectations)

2. **Involvement**
   - Active involvement of all students

3. **Success**
   - Reasonable activities that students can complete successfully.

4. **Scaffolding/cognitive strategies**
   - Visual organizers, adequate background information, and support provided by teachers to students by thinking aloud, building on and clarifying their input

5. **Mediation/feedback**
   - Strategies provided to students
   - Frequency and comprehensibility stressed

6. **Collaborative/cooperative learning**

7. **Techniques for second-language acquisition/sheltered English**
   - Extended discourse
   - Consistent language
   - Incorporation of students' language

8. **Respect for cultural diversity**
   - Respect and knowledge of cultural diversity

Additionally, **peer-mediated instruction** is effective in promoting higher levels of language and academic learning and social interaction. Research has shown that cooperative, peer-mediated instruction contributes more to content mastery than do whole-class instruction, workbook activities, and question-answer sessions. This method gives ELLs opportunities to actively practice a concept, the amount of discourse produced, the degree of negotiation of meaning, and the amount of comprehensible linguistic input. The essential components of peer-mediated learning strategies are: (a) cooperative incentives, (b) group rewards, (c) individual accountability, and (d) task structures.

In this method, students of varied academic abilities and language proficiency levels work together in pairs and small groups toward a common goal. In these groups, the success of one student depends on the help of the others. In peer-mediated instruction the learning task assigned to groups varies, but the format of learning always includes interaction and interdependence among the students.

Similarly, **peer tutoring** is a method developed to improve the acquisition and retention of basic academic skills. In this method, students are either paired randomly or matched by ability or language proficiency to partners each week. Student's roles are switched during the daily tutoring session, allowing each child to be both the tutor/teacher and the tutee/student. Students are trained in the procedures necessary to act as tutors and tutees. The four basic components of this method are:

- Weekly competing teams (culturally, linguistically, and ability-wise heterogeneous grouping)
- Highly structured teaching procedure (content material, teams, pairing, error correction, system of rewards)
- Daily, contingent, individual tutee point earning and public postings of individual and team scores
- Direct practice of functional academic and language skills to mastery

Academic tasks tend to increase in their cognitive demands as students progress in their schooling, but the context becomes increasingly reduced. ELLs who have not developed CALP need additional teacher support to achieve success. Contextual support in the form of realia, demonstrations, pictures, graphs, etc., provide the ELL with scaffolding and reduce the language difficulty level of the task. Both content and

ESOL teachers should incorporate teaching academic skills in their lessons. The following are essential elements to include in teaching academic English:

1. Integrate listening, speaking, reading, and writing skills in all lessons for all proficiencies.
2. Teach the components and processes of reading and writing.
3. Focus on vocabulary development.
4. Build and activate prior knowledge.
5. Teach language through content and themes.
6. Use native language strategically.
7. Pair technology with instruction.
8. Motivate ELLs with choice.

A number of program models have been developed to meet the needs of language minority students involving the integration of language and content instruction. In this approach, the second or foreign language is used as the medium of instruction for mathematics, science, social studies, and other academic subjects; it is the vehicle used for teaching and acquiring subject- specific knowledge. The focus of the second language classroom should be on something meaningful, such as academic content, and modification of the target language facilitates language acquisition and makes academic content accessible to second-language learners.

Integrated language-and-content instruction offers a means by which English as a Second Language (ESL) students can continue their academic or cognitive development while they are also acquiring academic language proficiency. In **theme-based programs,** a language curriculum is developed around selected topics drawn from one content area (e.g., marketing) or from across the curriculum (e.g., pollution and the environment). The theme could be a week or two long and focuses on language taught in a meaningful way. The goal is to assist learners in developing general academic language skills through interesting and relevant content. There are a variety of strategies to teach the integrated approach to language teaching of which the four most important are (Crandall, 1994):

1. **Cooperative learning:** In this method, students of different linguistic and educational backgrounds and different skill levels work together on a common task for a common goal to complete a task pertaining to the content being taught in the classroom. The focus is also on an implicit or explicit language feature that the students acquire through negotiation of meaning.
2. **Task-based or experiential learning:** Appropriate contexts are provided for developing thinking and study skills as well as language and academic concepts for students at different levels of language proficiency. Students learn by carrying out specific tasks or projects that they complete with a focus on the content, but learning language and academic skills as well.
3. **Whole language approach:** The philosophy of whole language is based on the concept that students need to experience language as an integrated whole. It focuses on the need for an integrated approach to language

instruction within a context that is meaningful to students (Goodman, 1986). The approach is consistent with integrated language and content instruction, as both emphasize meaningful engagement and authentic language use, and both link oral and written language development (Blanton, 1992). Whole language strategies that have been implemented in content-centered language classes include dialogue journals, reading response journals, learning logs, process-based writing, and language experience stories (Crandall, 1992).

4. **Graphic organizers:** These frameworks provide a "means for organizing and presenting information so that it can be understood, remembered, and applied" (Crandall, 1992). Graphs, realia, tables, maps, flow charts, timelines, and Venn diagrams are used to help students place information in a comprehensible context. These props enable students to organize information obtained from written or oral texts, develop reading strategies, increase retention, activate schema as a prereading or prelistening activity, and organize ideas during the prewriting stage (Crandall, 1992).

An approach to teach vocabulary and to build prior knowledge about the content for readers is the **language experience approach**. Pressley (2008) states that good readers make use of background knowledge to make inferences that are necessary for understanding a text. This process helps readers create new knowledge from the text (*top-down processing*). In light of this view, the language experience approach supports children's concept development and vocabulary growth while offering many opportunities for meaningful reading and writing activities. It also helps in the development of shared experiences that expand children's knowledge of the world around them. In this approach, students' attention is focused on an experience in their daily life such as taking a class walk to collect leaves, blowing bubbles, making popcorn, apple picking, or experimenting with magnets. Students are involved in planning, experiencing, responding to, and recording the experience. The teacher initiates a discussion eliciting narrative from the students while providing appropriate vocabulary. In the end, the students compose oral individual or group stories which the teacher writes down and reads with students.

Skill 10.2 Selection and adaptation of content area materials to address students' cognitive and linguistic needs

Sheltered instruction (SI) allows teachers to select and adapt content area materials in a way that addresses students' cognitive and linguistic needs. In sheltered classes, a core teacher instructs the students throughout the day. Teachers make grade-level content comprehensible by activating and building background knowledge. Teachers speak in clear, direct, simple English and use scaffolding techniques such as visuals, gestures, manipulatives, paraphrasing, etc. (i.e. anything that conveys the meaning to the EL). The classes have clear grade level, content, and language objectives.

Skill 10.3   Approaches for promoting the content area learning of English language learners at different ages, especially those who have experienced gaps and interruptions in their education

English language learners, who have had their education interrupted, face the dual challenge of learning grade-level content and learning the basic tenets which support grade-level content. For ELLs, the challenge is daunting as they must also learn English at the same time.

Some researchers believe there is a critical age at which the learners of a foreign language can maximize their learning. Penfield and Roberts (1959) expounded the theory of critical age in language learning based upon their studies of L1 and brain damage studies. Their studies showed that children who suffered brain damage before puberty typically recovered and develop normal language. Adults, however, rarely recover from such injuries and language remains fixed at the point of recovery reached 5 months after damage. Lenneberg (1967) supports Penfield and Roberts (1959) claim of neurological mechanisms responsible for maturational change in language learning abilities.

Chomsky's Universal Grammar (UG) suggests that language is an innate function of humans who have a language acquisition device (LAD) in their brains. The LAD allows children to construct a grammar out of raw input in their environment. Universal Grammar does not describe an optimal age for SLA, but the theory implies that the younger children learn languages more easily as their LAD is still active. Older learners loose this ability and rarely achieve complete fluency. Therefore, research suggests that UG may govern all languages, it becomes increasingly difficult for older learners to access their LAD and explicit instruction is needed to achieve language proficiency.

Piaget considers the brain to be computational device with language acquisition only one part of general learning. He believes that language is controlled by external influences and social interactions. The research of Newport and Supalla (1987) support Piaget's theories as their studies showed that language abilities decline with age just as other cognitive abilities do.

Both Krashen (1975) and Felix (1985) proposed theories for the close of the Critical Period of L2 at puberty based on Piaget's cognitive stage of formal operations beginning at puberty.

Cognitive processes are used by the learner to organize and direct second language acquisition. Examples of these processes are: problem-solving, method of approaching the learning of new information, and choices regarding what to ignore and what to notice (Díaz-Rico, Weed, 1995). Developing these skills leads to language acquisition, but these skills also bridge languages and serve to enhance cognition in the first language.

Research demonstrates that learning and using more than one language:

- Enhances problem solving and analytical skills
- Allows better formation of concepts
- Increases visual-social abilities
- Furthers logical reasoning
- Supports cognitive flexibility

Cognitive skills are any mental skills that are used in the process of acquiring knowledge, including reasoning, perception, and intuition. Using these skills in second-language learning applies L2 vocabulary and sentence patterns to thought processes that have already formed in the L1.

Memorizing the words and rules of a second language is insufficient to integrate the second language into the learner's thought patterns. L2 learners use cognitive processes to form rules, which allow them to understand and create novel utterances. The creation of novel utterances, whether grammatically correct or not, offers proof that the L2 learner is not simply mimicking chunks of prescribed language, but rather is using cognitive processes to acquire the second language. People use their own thinking processes, or cognition, to discover the rules of the language they are acquiring.

Planning what actions to take when confronted with an academic (or social) challenge demonstrates understanding of the problem and the ability to confront it. By engaging the cognitive skills, the student can plan where and how to search for information, how to organize it and how to present the information for review.

Organizational skills may show differences in different cultural contexts. For example, when organizing information for writing, the English speaker normally goes from a smaller unit to a larger unit. In addresses, for example:

Dr. Randal Price
Department of English as a Second Language
University of Georgia
Athens, Ga.
USA.

A Japanese speaker would begin with the larger unit and go to the smaller one. For example:

USA
Athens, Ga.
University of Georgia
Department of English as a Second Language
Dr. Randal Price

Teachers cannot assume their students know these skills. Even the most basic organizational skill concepts must be glossed or fully taught if necessary.

Skill 10.4 **Characteristics of and guidelines for using various formal and informal procedures and instruments for assessing students' cognitive-academic language proficiency and content area concepts and skills and interpretation and use of assessment information, including differentiation between normal variation in performance and performance that may indicate possible learning disabilities**

Students in Massachusetts are required to participate in both the **Massachusetts Comprehensive Assessment System (MCAS)** which tests students' academic performance based on the Massachusetts Curriculum Frameworks **and** the **Massachusetts English Proficiency Assessment (MEPA)** which tests students' English language proficiency based on the English Language Proficiency Benchmarks and Outcomes (Vohs, 2009).

The MCAS tests each public school student in Massachusetts in English Language Arts and mathematics each year in grades 3-8 and once in high school. Students must also take a science and engineering/technology test once in elementary, middle, and high school (Vohs, 2009). The testing schedule as of 2011 does not include History and Social Science because of budget constraints. All ELLs must take the tests. Exceptions are those in their first year of schooling in the U.S. are not required to test in English Language Arts. However, they must test in Mathematics and Science & Technology/Engineering.

The MEPA is a series of tests that measure the proficiency of ELLs in the study of the English language. The tests are broken down into:

- **MELA-O (Massachusetts English Language Assessment-Oral):** Given to ELLs in K-12. The test measures both speaking and listening. Each ELL is observed in the actual classroom and scored by a qualified MELA-O assessor based on his/her ability to understand and speak English.
- **MEPA-R/W (Massachusetts English Proficiency Assessment – Reading and Writing):** The test measures proficiency in reading and writing based on the reading component and the writing component.

Most students take the tests in the spring, but those who were not tested the previous spring, will take the test in the fall. When the ELL becomes proficient in English, he/she is reclassified as Former Limited English Proficient (FLEP). The FLEP is still required to take the MEPA in the spring of the current school year.

Students with disabilities are allowed special accommodations, if any, as specified in their IEPs or 504 plans.

DISTINCTION BETWEEN ELL AND STUDENTS WITH DISABILITIES

One way to serve the student with disabilities and the ELL student is to accurately assess their disability or limitation. How can teachers differentiate between ELLs with learning disabilities from those who are simply struggling with learning a second language? It is not easy. Many of the problems associated with second language learning are also identified as learning difficulties: for example, should processing difficulties, behavioral differences, reading difficulties, and expressive difficulties (Lock & Layton, 2002) be associated with the difficulties of second language learning or learning difficulties? While some learning difficulties can be partially identified by observation over a period of time or by the lack of academic improvement (Gersten & Baker, 2003) they are also typical of ELLs struggling with the complexities of language and a new school environment.

Therefore, it is of critical importance to assess the concerned student using a variety of testing procedures. Chalfant & Psch (1981) recommend using a Teacher Assistance Team (TAT) consisting of regular classroom teachers who meet with the referring teacher to discuss problems, brainstorm possible solutions, and develop an action plan. After the plan has been implemented, the TAT and the referring teacher have a follow-up meeting to evaluate the results and to develop other recommendations if necessary. The TAT ultimately decides whether or not the student should be referred for a special education evaluation.

Suggestions concerning the testing procedure are:

- Tests that are nondiscriminatory based on race or culture
- Tests conducted in both the student's primary language and English
- Identify student using observations from school, home, and community
- Alternative assessments combined with formal assessments
- Criterion-referenced assessments
- Curriculum-based assessments
- Portfolio of student's work
- Informal assessments: rubrics, dynamic assessment (test-teach-test), learning logs, self-evaluations
- Comparison of student's cultural teaching style (teacher centered, e.g.) with the school's teaching style (student centered, e.g.)

Further Reading on ELLs with Disabilities

A major obstacle in working with ELLs with disabilities is the lack of guidelines dealing specifically with the two limitations. While both learning disabilities and teaching English to minorities or immigrants have been studied extensively, little research has been done on how to best integrate the two disciplines (Gersten & Baker, 2003; Ortiz, 1997 in Gurel 2004). The following suggestions for further reading are offered to those who wish more enlightenment.

- Aron, L.Y. & Loprest, P.J. (2007) Meeting the Needs of Children with Disabilities. Urban Institute Press.
- Echevarria, J. & Graves, A. (1998) Sheltered content Instruction: Teaching English-Language Learners with Diverse Abilities. Allyn and Bacon. .
- Wynne, S. 2011. Praxis 0353. Special Education: Knowledge-Based Core Principles. Teacher Certification Exam. Boston: XAMonline.
- Zehr, Mary Ann (2008) "Bilingual Students with Disabilities Get Special Help." *Education Week*. Nov. 7, 2001.
- http://www.eric.ed.gov/
- http://www.edweek.org/ew/articles/2001/11/07/10clark.h21.html?print=1
- http://learningdisabilities.about.com

Changes in Requirements for IEPs

Individualized Education Plans (IEPS) continue to have multiple sections. One section, *present levels of educational performance (PLEP),* now addresses *academic achievement and functional performance.* Annual IEP goals must now address the same areas.

IEP goals should be aligned to state standards, therefore, short term objectives are not required on every IEP. Students with IEPs must not only participate in regular education programs to the full extent possible, they must also show progress in those programs. Therefore, goals must be written to reflect academic progress.

For students who must participate in alternate assessment, there must be alignment to *alternate achievement standards.*

Significant change has been made in the definition of the IEP team. It now states that *not less than 1* teacher from each of the areas of special education and regular education be present.

IDEA 2004 recognized that the amount of required paperwork placed upon teachers of students with disabilities should be reduced if possible. For this reason, some states will participate in a newly developed pilot program that uses multi-year IEPs. Individual student inclusion in this program will require consent by both the school and the parent.

IDENTIFICATION

Identification of a student's learning problem occurs when comparisons are made between a given student's academic and behavioral characteristics and those of the peer population. Teachers hold expectations for student behaviors, and those who exhibit actions that differ are singled out.

All children and youth exhibit behaviors that deviate from normative expectations at times. But overall, it is the intensity of the behavior, the degree to which it is shown, and the frequency and length of time that it persists or has occurred that is significant. Behavior rating scales, checklists, inventories, and sociograms are used to determine whether a particular behavior is occurring and to what extent.

Students with disabilities are identifiable by academic and social behaviors that deviate significantly from those of their classmates. The longer it takes to identify these students, the further they fall behind their age-mates in school.

INTERVENTION

Once a student is identified as being at-risk academically or socially, remedial interventions are attempted within the regular classroom. Federal legislation requires that sincere efforts be made to help the child learn in the regular classroom.

In some states, school-based teams of educators are formed to solve learning and behavior problems in the regular classroom. These informal problem-solving teams have a variety of names that include concepts of support (school support teams, student support teams), assistance (teacher assistant teams, school assistance teams, or building assistance teams), and appraisal (school appraisal teams) (Pugach & Johnson 1989b).

Regardless of what the teams are called, their purpose is similar. Chalfant, Pysh, and Moultrie (1979) state that **teacher assistance teams (TAT)** are created to make professional suggestions about curricular alternatives and instructional modifications. These teams may be composed of a variety of participants, including regular education teachers including ESOL teachers, building administrators, guidance counselors, special education teachers, and the student's parent(s). The make-up of teams varies based on the type of referral, the needs of the student, and availability of educational personnel and state requirements.

Instructional modifications are tried in an attempt to accommodate the student in the regular classroom. Effective instruction is geared toward individual needs and recognizes differences in how students learn. Modifications are tailored to individual student needs. Some strategies for modifying regular classroom instruction shown in the table below are effective with at-risk students with disabilities and students without learning or behavior problems.

REFERRAL

Referral is the process through which a teacher, a parent, or some other person formally requests an evaluation of a student to determine eligibility for special education services. The decision to refer a student may be influenced by the following:

- Student characteristics, such as the abilities, behaviors, or skills (or lack thereof) that students exhibit;
- Individual differences among teachers, in their beliefs, expectations, or skill in dealing with specific kinds of problems;
- Expectations for assistance with a student who is exhibiting academic or behavioral learning problems;

- Availability of specific kinds of strategies and materials;
- Parents' request for referral or opposition to referral; and
- Institutional factors that may facilitate or constrain teachers in making referral decisions. Fewer students are referred when school districts have complex procedures for referral, psychological assessments are backlogged for months, special education classes are filled to capacity, or principals and other administrators do not fully recognize the importance of special services.

Everyone must clearly understand referral procedures, and they must be coordinated among all school personnel. All educators must to be able to identify characteristics typically exhibited by special needs students. Also, the restrictiveness of special service settings must be known and the appropriateness of each clearly understood. The more restrictive special education programs tend to group students with similar disabilities for instruction. Last, the specialized services afforded through equipment, materials, teaching approaches, and specific teacher-student relations should be clearly understood.

EVALUATION

If instructional modifications in the regular classroom have not proven successful, a student may be referred for multidisciplinary evaluation. The evaluation is comprehensive and includes:

- Norm and criterion-referenced tests (e.g., IQ and diagnostic tests)
- Curriculum-based assessment
- Systematic teacher observation (e.g., behavior frequency checklist)
- Samples of student work
- Parent interviews

The purpose of the evaluation is twofold: to determine eligibility for special education services and to identify a student's strengths and weaknesses in order to plan an individual education program.

The wording in federal law is very explicit about the manner in which evaluations must be conducted and about the existence of due process procedures that protect against bias and discrimination. Provisions in the law include the following:

- The testing of children in their native or primary language unless it is clearly not feasible to do so
- The use of evaluation procedures selected and administered to prevent cultural or ethnic discrimination.
- The use of assessment tools validated for the purpose for which they are being used (e.g., achievement levels, IQ scores, adaptive skills)
- Assessment by a multidisciplinary team using several pieces of information to formulate a placement decision

Furthermore, parental involvement must occur in the development of the child's educational program. According to the law, parents must:

- Be notified before initial evaluation or any change in placement by a written notice in their primary language describing the proposed school action, the reasons for it, and the available educational opportunities
- Consent, in writing, before the child is initially evaluated

Parents may then:

- Request an independent educational evaluation if they feel the school's evaluation is inappropriate
- Request an evaluation at public expense if a due process hearing decision is that the public agency's evaluation was inappropriate
- Participate on the committee that considers the evaluation, placement, and programming of the student

All students referred for evaluation for special education should have on file the results of a relatively current vision and hearing screening. This will determine the adequacy of sensory acuity and ensure that learning problems are not due to a vision and/or hearing problem.

ELIGIBILITY

Eligibility is based on criteria defined in federal law or state regulations, which vary from state to state. Evaluation methods correspond with eligibility criteria for the special education classifications. For example, a multidisciplinary evaluation for a student being evaluated for intellectual disabilities would include the individual's intellectual functioning, adaptive behavior, and achievement levels. Other tests are based on developmental characteristics exhibited (e.g., social, language, and motor).

A student evaluated for learning disabilities is given reading, math, and spelling achievement tests, an intelligence test to confirm average or above average cognitive capabilities, and tests of written and oral language ability. Tests need to show a discrepancy between potential and performance. Classroom observations and samples of student work (such as impaired reading ability or impaired writing ability) also provide indicators of possible learning disabilities.

Eligibility for services in behavior disorders requires documented evidence of social deficiencies or learning deficits that are not because of intellectual, sensory, or physical conditions. Therefore, any student undergoing multidisciplinary evaluation for this categorical service is usually given an intelligence test, diagnostic achievement tests, and social and/or adaptive inventories. Results of behavior frequency lists, direct observations, and anecdotal records collected over an extended period often accompany test results.

Additional information frequently used when making decisions about a child's eligibility for special education include the following:

- Developmental history
- Past academic performance
- Medical history or records
- Neurological reports
- Classroom observations
- Speech and language evaluations
- Personality assessment
- Discipline reports
- Home visits
- Parent interviews
- Samples of student work

If considered eligible for special education services, the child's disability should be documented in a written report stating specific reasons for the decision.

Three-year reevaluations (Triennials) of a student's progress are required by law and determine the growth and changing needs of the student. During the re-evaluation, continued eligibility for services in special education must be assessed using a range of evaluation tools similar to those used during the initial evaluation. All relevant information about the student is considered when making a decision about continued eligibility or whether the student no longer needs the service and is ready to begin preparing to exit the program. If the student is deemed ready to exit the program, then planning for the transition must occur.

DOMAIN IV   ENGLISH LANGUAGE ORAL PROFICIENCY

The sample questions that follow illustrate the kinds of questions on the MTEL test. They are not, however, representative of the entire scope of the test either in content or in difficulty.

Directions: In this part of the actual test, you will hear and read a series of short prompts. Then you will be asked to construct an oral response similar to the written ones provided below. These responses are to be used only as guides.

COMPETENCY 11.0   IN A RESPONSE TO A PROMPT ON TAPE AND IN WRITING, THE CANDIDATE WILL CONSTRUCT CONNECTED ORAL DISCOURSE IN STANDARD ENGLISH THAT COMMUNICATES A MESSAGE EFFECTIVELY AND THAT DEMONSTRATES A COMMAND OF VOCABULARY AND SYNTAX APPROPRIATE TO AN EDUCATIONAL SETTING

Skill 11.1   Narrate an event

When I was a child, my parents took me to visit the zoo. We walked around for hours looking at the different animals. The first exhibits were the birds and the butterfly exhibits. The birds screeched and flittered back and forth. The tropical birds were beautiful. Next, we saw the giant tortoises from the Galapagos Islands. They looked like huge stones. I don't remember which animals we saw next, but I was so excited that I kept running ahead of my parents.

The animals seemed excited to see us .They frolicked and paced back and forth in their cages. Years later, when I went to the zoo again with my little cousins, I could see that the zoo had changed considerably, and for the better. The animals were in free-roaming enclosures and were lying around on the ground. I realized that keeping wild animals in cages was cruel to these magnificent creatures. However, as a child, I was enchanted and thought the zoo was a marvelous place.

Skill 11.2   Discuss the advantages and disadvantages of an idea or proposed course of action

Recently, on our campus, it was suggested that we eliminate sports in favor of more academics. I think this is a terrible idea. I enjoy sports and everyone needs to develop a sport as a means of keeping fit for life and to have a hobby to enjoy. I personally like tennis and I plan to keep playing after I finish my schooling.

The only advantage of this idea, that I can see, is that some jocks would have no excuse for not achieving academic excellence. This is good. Sometimes, these guys get so involved in their sport during the season, that they forget that collegiate competitive sports lead to very few college students going on to the pros. Most of these guys will need their college degree to get a good job, and so they should be concentrating on their studies, not giving priority to sports.

Skill 11.3   Respond to a hypothetical situation by describing events or circumstances or by proposing a solution to a problem

Example 1: Describing Events or Circumstances
Recently, I was stopped by a police car. I was pretty sure that I hadn't done anything wrong, but it scared me to see the police car, lights flashing in my rearview mirror.

I was driving my boyfriend to the airport. I stopped at a traffic light and made a left turn when the left-hand arrow turned on. I was getting on an expressway when the lights began to flash behind me.
I didn't know what to do. I had not even seen a police car anywhere around the intersection. I knew if I got on the expressway, it would be dangerous to stop on the edge because this section was an elevated highway with very narrow shoulders and rapid traffic. I waited for everyone to go around me and I edged back onto the access highway and the right lane. I was signaling with my blinker all the time.

When the policeman came up to my window, I stuttered, "What did I do wrong?" He replied by asking for my license, and went to run my plate number and driver's license number. He came back and he told me one of my taillights was out. He gave me a courtesy ticket and said I should get the taillight fixed as soon as possible. Was I ever relieved.

or

Example 2: Proposing a Solution to a Problem
When I was doing my undergraduate practice teaching, I wanted my students to learn how to use their English in a more fun way. Often the textbook exercises seemed boring to them, so I decided to try something new. I found a wonderful book in the library called Recipes for Writing. I liked the writing prompts they gave and decided to try them out. One was called Alphabet Stories. In this exercise, the students write a fairy tale using only 26 sentences, one for each letter of the alphabet. I helped them with the language when they got stuck on letters like "q" and 'z", but they enjoyed the exercise and found it really challenging. It was so much fun that I decided to use other "recipes" in my classes whenever I could.

REFERENCES

Alderson, J. 1992. Guidelines for the evaluation of language education. In: Ellis, R. 1997. The empirical evaluation of language teaching materials. ELT Journal Vol. 51, No. 1 Jan.

Allen, V.G. (1994) Selecting materials for the instruction of ESL children. In: Zainuddin (2007).

Au, K. H. 1993. Literacy instruction in multicultural settings. Orlando, FL.: Harcourt Brace.

------ 2002. Multicultural factors and effective instruction of students of diverse backgrounds. In A. Farstrup and S. J. Samuels (eds.) *What research says about reading Instruction.* Newark, DE: International Reading Assn. Coral Gables: U of Miami. 392-413.

Banks, J. A. 1988. Multicultural Leader. Vol. 1, No. 2. Educational Materials & Services Center. Spring.

Baker, K. 1998. Structured English Immersion: Breakthrough in Teaching Limited-English-Proficient Students. Phi Delta Kappan, Nov. pp199-204.

Barton, L. 1997. Quick Flip Questions for Critical Thinking. Dana Point, CA: Edupress.

Bebe, V.N & Mackey, W.F. 1990. *Bilingual schooling and the Miami experience.* Coral Gables, FL University of Miami. Institute of Interamerican Studies. Graduate School of International Studies.

Bennett, C. 1995. Comprehensive multicultural education: Theory and practice (3rd ed.). Massachusetts: Allen & Bacon.

Berko Gleason, J. 1993. *The Development of Language* (3rd ed.) New York: Macmillan.

Bialystok, E. (ed.). 1991. *Language Processing in Bilingual Children.* Cambridge: CUP.

Blakey, E. & Spence, S. 1990. Developing Metacognition (ED327218). ERIC Clearinghouse on Information Resources. Syracuse, NY.

Brisk, M. E. 1998. Bilingual Education: From compensatory to quality schooling. Mahwah, N. J. Lawrence Erlbaum.

Burstall, C., Jamieson, M., Cohen, S. and Hargreaves, M. 1974. *Primary French I the balance*. Slough: NFER.

California Department of Education. Testing & Accountability. CELDT Questions and Answers. http://www.cde.ca.gov/ta/tg/el/celdtfaq.asp Rev. 11/03/09.

Candlin, C. 1987. In Batstone, R. 1994. *Grammar*. Oxford: OUP.

Chalfant, J.C. & Pysh, M.V. 1981. Teacher assistance teams—A model for within building problem solving. Counterpoint. Nov. p 16-21.

Chalfant, J.C., Pysh, M.V. & Moultrie, R. 1979. Teacher Assistance Teams: A Model for Within-Building Problem Solving. Learning Disability Quarterly. v2, n3 Summer, p. 85-96. Council for Learning Disabilities.

Chamot, A.U. and O'Malley, J. M. 1994. *The Calla Handbook*. Reading, MA: Addison-Wesley.

Collier, V.P. 1989. "How long? A synthesis of research on academic achievement in second language." *TESOL Quarterly*, 23. 509-531.

-----. 1992. A synthesis of studies examining long-term language minority student data on academic achievement. *Bilingual Research Journal*, 16 (1-2). 187-212.

-----. 1995. "Acquiring a second language for school." Directions in Language & Education. Washington, DC: NCBE. 1(4), 1-10.
Conflict Research Consortium. Online Training Program on Intractable Conflict (OTPIC) Conflict Management and Constructive Confrontation: A Guide to the Theory and Practice. University of Colorado Revised July 20, 1999. http://conflict.colorado.edu
Crawford, J. 1998. Ten Common Fallacies About Bilingual Education. ERIC Clearinghouse on Language & Linguistics . Washington, D.C. Nov. ERIC Id ED424792.

Criteria for Evaluating Instructional Materials: Kindergarten Through Grade Eight. Reading/Language Arts Framework for California Public Schools. California Department of Education. 2007.

Cruz, J. 2005. Second Language Acquisition Programs: An Assessment of the Bilingual Education Debate. McNair Scholars Journal: Vol. 9, Iss. 1, Art. 6. http://scholarworks.gvsu.edu/mcnair/vol/iss1/6

Cummins, J. 1981. Bilingualism and Minority Language Children. Toronto: Institute for Studies in Education.

Cummins, J. 1984. Bilingualism and special education: Issues in assessment and pedagogy. San Diego: College-Hill.

Cummins, J. 1998. Rossell and Baker: Their case for the effectiveness of bilingual education. The Journal of Pedagogy Pluralism & Practice. Issue 3, Vol. 1: Fall.

Cummins, J. & Genzuk, M. 1991. Analysis of final report longitudinal study of structured English immersion strategy, early-exit and late-exit transitional bilingual education programs for language-minority students. California Association for Bilingual Education Newsletter, 13.

Curry, D. 1989. Illustrated American Idioms. Washington, DC. English Language Program Division. Bureau of Educational and Cultural Affairs. USIA.

Díaz-Rico, L.T. and Weed, K.Z. 1995. Language, and Academic Development Handbook: A Complete K-12 Reference Guide. Needham Heights, MA: Allyn and Bacon.

Diaz-Rico, L.T. 2008. Strategies for Teaching English Learners. 2nd ed. Boston: Pearson.

Dulay, H. and Burt, M. 1974. "You can't learn without goofing" in J. Richards' (ed.) Error Analysis, Perspectives on Second Language Acquisition. New York: Longman.

Ellis, R. 1985. Understanding Second Language Acquisition. Oxford: OUP.

------ 1994. The Study of Second Language Acquisition. Oxford: OUP.

Entwhistle, N.J. and Entwhistle, D. 1970. The relationships between personality, study methods and academic performance. British Journal of Educational Psychology. Vol 40(2). doi.apa.org. 132-143.

Fillmore, L.W. 2001. Scott, Foresman ESL:Accelerating English Language Learning. In: Zainuddin (2007).

Friend, M. and Bursuck, W. D. 2005. *Models of Coteaching: Including Students with Special Needs: A Practical Guide for Classroom Teachers*. (3rd ed.) Boston, MA: Allyn and Bacon.

Garcia, E. 1994. *Understanding and Meeting the Challenge of Student Cultural Diversity*. Boston: Houghton Mifflin.

Garinger, D. 2002. Textbook Evaluation. TESL Web Journal Vol. 1, No. 3.

Genesee, F. 1987. *Learning through Two Languages: Studies of Immersion and Bilingual Education*. Cambridge, MA: Newbury House.

------ (ed.) 1994. *Educating Second Language Children: The Whole Child, the Whole Curriculum, the Whole Community*. Cambridge: CUP.

Grellet, F. 1981. *Developing Reading Skills*. Cambridge: CUP.

Gersten, R. & Baker, S. 2000. What we know about effective instructional practices for English-Language Learners. Exceptional Children, 66(4) June, p. 454-470.

Gersten, R. & Baker, S. 2003. English-Language Learners with Learning Disabilities. In H. L. Swanson, K. R. Harris & S. Graham (eds.) Handbook of Learning Disabilities. (pp. 94-109). NY: Guilford.

Grasha, A. F. 1996. Your teaching style. Pittsburgh, PA: International Alliance of Teacher Scholars.

Gregorc, A.1982. An adult's guide to style. Maynard, MA: Gabriel Systems.

Gurel, Sarah M. (2004) Teaching English Language Learners with Learning Disabilities: A Compiled Convergence of Strategies. College of William and Mary. School of Education, Curriculum and Instruction.

Harris, M. and McCann, P. 1994. *Assessment*. Oxford: Heinemann.
Jerald, C.D. 2006. School Culture: "The Hidden Curriculum". The Center for Comprehensive School Reform and Improvement. Issue Brief. December. www.centerforcsri.org

Heywood, D. 2006. Using Whole Discourse Tasks for Language Teaching. www.jalt-publications.org/tlt/chaprep/ Jan.

Hruska-Reichmann, S. & Grasha, A.F. 1982. The Grasha-Reichmann Student Learning Scales: Research findings and applications. In. J. Keefe (Ed.). Student learning styles and brain behavior. Reston, VA: NASSP.

Hyland, K. 2002. Teaching and Researching Writing. Harlow, England: Pearson.
Keirsey, D. 1998. Please understand me II. Del Mar, CA: Prometheus Nemesis.

Kolb, D. A. 1976. The learning style Inventory technical manual. Boston: McBer.

Kramsch, C. 1998. *Language and Culture*. Oxford: OUP.

Krashen, S. 1981. *Second Language Acquisition and Second Language Learning*. Oxford: Pergamon Press.

------1982. *Principles and Practice in Second Language Acquisition*. Oxford: Pergamon Press.

Lambert, W. and Klineberg, O. 1967. Children's views of foreign peoples: A crossnational study. New York: Appleton. (Review in Shumann, J., Affective factors and the problem of age in second language acquisition, *Language Learning* 25/2. 1975. 209-235).

Lambert, W. E. 1990. Issues in Foreign Language and Second Language Education. In: Proceedings of the Research Symposium on Limited English Proficient Students' Issues. (1st, Washington, DC. September 10-12. ED 341 269. FI 020 030.

Larsen, D. and Smalley, W. 1972. *Becoming Bilingual, a Guide to Language Learning.* New Canadian: CT. Practical Anthropology.

Larsen-Freeman, D. 1997. Chaos/complexity science and second language acquisition. *Applied Linguistics*, 18 (2). 141-165.

Leshinsky, J.G. 1995. Authentic listening and discussion for advanced students. Englewood Cliffs, NJ: Prentice-Hall Regents.

Lock, R.H. & Layton, C. A. 2002. Isolating Intrinsic Processing Disorders from Second Language Acquisition. Bilingual Research Journal. v 26n2 p. 383-94. Summer

Long, M. 1990. The lease a second language acquisition theory needs to explain. *TESOL Quarterly*. 24(4). 649-666.

The Map of Standards for ELS. 2002. 3rd ed. West Education.

McArthur, T. ed. 1992. *The Oxford Companion to the English Language*. Oxford: OUP. 571-573.

McCarthy, B. 1983. The 4-MAT system: Teaching to learning styles with right-left mode techniques. Oak Brook, IL: Excel.

McClelland, D., Atkinson, J., Clark, R. & Lowell, E. 1953. *The Achievement Motive.* New York: Appleton, Century, Crofts.

McDonough, J. and Shaw, S. 1993. *Materials and Methods in ELT: A Teacher's Guide.* Blackwell.

McKay, S. L. 1987. Teaching Grammar: form, function, and technique. New York: Prentice Hall.

McLaughlin, B. 1990. The development of bilingualism: Myth and reality. In A. Barona & E. Garcia (eds.) *Children at Risk: Poverty, Minority Status and other Issues in Educational Equity* . Washington, D.C.: National Association of School Psychologists. 65-76.

Mitchell, V. 1990. Curriculum and instruction to reduce racial conflict. (ED322274). ERIC Clearinghouse on Urban Education. NY, NY.

Murphy, J. M. 1998. The eight disciplines. Grand Rapids, MI: Venture Management.

Naiman, N., Frolich, M., Stern, H., and Todesco, A. 1978. *The Good Language Learner.* Toronto: The Modern Language Centre, Ontario Institute for Studies in Education.

National Center for Research on Cultural Diversity and Second Language Learning. 1999. Two-Way Bilingual Education Programs in Practice: A National and Local Perspective. Center for Applied Linguistics, Online Resources: Digest. July.

National Center on Education and the Economy. 2001. California Performance Standards.

Nieto, S. 1992. "We Have Stories to Tell: A Case Study of Puerto Ricans in Children's Books." In Harris, V.J. (Ed.), Teaching Multicultural Literature in Grades K-8. Norwood, MA: Christopher-Gordon Publishers.

Nunan, D. 1989. *Designing Tasks for the Communicative Classroom.* Cambridge, CUP.

O'Malley, J. M. and Pierce, L. V. 1996. *Authentic Assessment for English Language Learners.* Longman.

Ovando, C.J., Coombs, M.C., and Collier, V.P. eds. 2006. *Bilingual and ESL Classrooms: Teaching in Multicultural Contexts* (4th ed.) Boston: McGraw-Hill.

Oxford, R. 2001. Integrated skills in the ESL/EFL classroom. Center for Applied Linguistics. Online Digests. Sept. EDO-FL-01-05.

Penfield, W. and Roberts, L. 1959. *Speech and Brain Mechanisms.* New York: Atheneum Press. (reviewed in Ellis, R. 1985).

Peregoy, S.F. and Boyle, O.F. 2008 *Reading, Writing, and Learning in ESL. 5th ed.* Boston: Pearson.

Prabhu, N. S. 1987. *Second Language Pedagogy: A Perspective.* London: Oxford, OUP.

Pugach, M.C. & Johnson, L.J. 1989. The Challenge of Implementing Collaboration between General and Special Education. Exceptional Children. V56.

Pugach, M.C. & Johnson, L.J. 1989. Prereferral Interventions: Progress, Problems, and Challenges. Exceptional Children. V56.

Quiocho, A. and Ulanoff, S.H. 2009. Differentiated Literacy Instruction for English Language Learners. Boston: Allyn & Bacon.

Reading/Language Arts Framework for California Public Schools. Kindergarten through Grade Twelve. 1999. Sacramento: CA DOE.

Reid, J. The learning style preferences of ESL students. *TESOL Quarterly,* 21(1): 86-103.

Rennie, J. 1993. ESL and Bilingual Program Models. Eric Digest.
http://www.cal.org/resources/Digest/rennie01.html

Richards, Platt, and Weber. 1985. quoted by Ellis, R. The evaluation of communicative tasks in Tomlinson, B (ed.) *Materials Development in Language Teaching.* Cambridge: CUP. 1998.

Rinvolucri, M. 1984. Grammar Games: Cognitive, affective and movement activities for EFL students. Cambridge, CUP.

Rinvolucri, M. and Davis, P. 1995. More Grammar Games: Cognitive, affective and movement activities for EFL students. Cambridge, CUP.

Rochman, H. 1993. Against Borders: Promoting Books for a Multicultural World. Chicago, IL: American Library Association.

Rosansky, E. 1975. The critical period for the acquisition of language: some cognitive developmental considerations. In: Working Papers on Bilingualism 6: 92-102.

Rosenberg, L. Global Demographic Trends. F&D: Finance and Development Sept. 2006, Vol. 43, No. 3.

Rosenblatt, L. 2005. Making meaning with texts: selected essays. Portsmouth, NH: Heinemann.

Samway, K.D. & McKeon, D. 1999. Myths and realities: Best practices for language minority students. Portsmouth, NH: Heinemann.

Schiffrin, D., Tannen, D., and Hamilton, H., eds. 2003. The Handbook of Discourse Analysis. Wiley, John & Sons.

Schimel, J. et al 2000. Running from the Shadow: Psychological Distancing From Others to Characteristics People Fear in Themselves. Journal of Personality and Social Psychology. Vol. 78, No. 3 446-462

Schmidt, R. W. 1990. The role of consciousness in second language acquisition. *Applied Linguistics*, 11(2). 129-158.

Schumm, J.S., ed. 2006. *Reading Assessment and Instruction for All Learners*. New York: The Guilford Press.

Sinclair, J. and Coulthard, M. 1975. Towards an Analysis of Discourse. Oxford: OUP. 93-94.

Slavin, R.E. and Cheung. 2003. *Effective Reading Programs for English Language Learners: A Best-Evidence Synthesis*. U.S. Dept. of Education. Institute of Education Sciences.

Snow, C. and Hoefnagel-Hohle, M. 1978. Age Differences in Second Language Learning. In *Second Language Acquisition,* Hatch ed. Rowley, MA.: Newbury House.

Sonbuchner, G. M. 1991. How to take advantage of your learning styles. Syracuse, NY: New Readers Press. .

Suid, M. & Lincoln, W. 1989. Recipes for Writing: Motivation, Skills, and Activities. Menlo Park, CA Addison-Wesley.

Taylor, O.L. 1990. Cross-Cultural Communication An Essential Dimension of Effective Education. Rev. ed. Chevy Chase, MD. Mid-Atlantic Equity Center.

Teachers of English to Speakers of Other Languages. 1997. *ESL Standards for Pre-K—12 Students*. Alexandria, VA.: TESOL.

Teaching Tolerance. n.d. *Anti-Gay Discrimination In Schools*. Southern Poverty Law Center, (http://www.tolerance.org)

Tharp, R. 1989. Psychocultural variables and constants: Effects on teaching and learning in schools. American Psychologist, 44(2). 349-359.

Thomas, W. P., and Collier, V. P. 1995. Language minority student achievement and program effectiveness. Manuscript in preparation. (in Collier, V.P. 1995).

Tollefsen, J. 1991. *Planning Language, Planning Inequality*. New York, Longman.

Tompkins, G. 2009. *Language Arts: patterns of practice*. 7th ed. Upper Saddle River, N.J.: Pearson.

Traugott, E. C. and Pratt, M. L. 1980. *Linguistics for Students of Literature*. San Diego: Harcourt Brace Jovanovich.

Trim, J.M. 1981. Council of Europe Educational Objectives. Adapted from the report of a working party of the British National Congress on Languages in Education.

Two-Way Immersion Education: the Basics. 2005. Center for Applied Linguistics. http://www.alliance.brown.edu/pubs/twi and http://www.cal.org/twi

United Nations Cyberschoolbus. 1996. Understanding Discrimination. cyberschoolbus@un.org

Unrau, N. 2008. *Content Area Reading and Writing.* 2nd ed. Upper Saddle River, N.J.: Pearson.

Ur, P. 1996. *A Course in Language Teaching.* Cambridge: CUP.

Valsiner, J. 2003. Culture and its Transfer: Ways of Creating General Knowledge Through the Study of Cultural Particulars. In W. J. Lonner, D. L. Dinnel, S. A. Hayes, & D. N. Sattler (Eds.), Online Readings in Psychology and Culture (Unit 2, Chapter 12), (http://www.wwu.edu/~culture), Center for Cross-Cultural Research, Western Washington University, Bellingham, Washington.

Vohs, J. 2009. Parents Place Pointers. Massachusetts Parent Information & Resource Center (PIRC). Northhampton, MA.

Vygotsky, L.S. 1986. *Thought and language.* Cambridge, MA: MIT Press.

Vygotsky, L.S. 2006. *Mind in society.* Cambridge, MA: Harvard University Press.

Watson, S. (2011) Learning Disability Checklist. www.About.com

Weir, C. 1993. *Understanding and Developing Language Tests.* Hemel Hempstead: Prentice Hall International.

Willing, K. 1988. "Learning strategies as information management: Some definitions for a theory of learning strategies". *Prospect* 3/2: 139-55.

Yokota, J. 1993." Issues in Selecting Multicultural Children's Literature." Language Arts, 70, 156-167.

Zainuddin, H., et al. 2007. *Fundamentals of Teaching English to Speakers of Other Languages in K-12 Mainstream Classrooms.* 2nd ed. Dubuque: Kendall/Hunt.

Zebroski, J. T. 1994. Thinking through theory: Vygotskian perspectives on the teaching of writing. Portsmouth, NH: Boynton/Cook.

Zwiers, J. 2007. *Building Academic Language. Essential Practices for Content Classrooms, Grades 5-12.* San Francisco: Jossey-Bass.

Sample Test

1. **ELLs who are practicing listening skills might be asked to:**
   (Average) (Skill 1.1)

   A. record their voice
   B. listen to the TV
   C. summarize a listening selection in a journal
   D. audio tape a passage from a TV program, radio, or native speaker

2. **An effective way to teach students to actively listen for information would be:**
   (Rigorous) (Skill 1.2)

   A. asking comprehension questions after completing a listening activity
   B. frontloading vocabulary
   C. provide a graphic organizer to be filled in during the listening activity
   D. quiz

3. **Students need to monitor their listening strategies because:**
   (Average) (Skill 1.2)

   A. monitoring is an ineffective learning strategy
   B. the ELL needs to work on self-improvement strategies
   C. monitoring listening activities helps ELLs see their mistakes
   D. not all strategies are effective

4. **All of the following are reasons an ELL will not respond in a listening class except:**
   (Average) (Skill 1.3)

   A. feels the class is a waste of his/her time
   B. has nothing to say
   C. doesn't know what to say
   D. is embarrassed to admit they didn't understand

5. **A major factor in reluctance to speak in language class is:**
   (Average) (Skill 1.3)

   A. voice
   B. anxiety
   C. gestures
   D. mime

6. **All of the following are examples of BICS except:**
   (Average) (Skill 1.3)

   A. Call me.
   B. Text me after the game.
   C. Work on problems 1-5.
   D. Please give me a fruit salad and a glass of milk.

7. **Which one of the following activities encourages paraphrasing skills?**
   (Easy) (Skill 1.4)

   A. Condensing a paragraph
   B. Explaining a math problem
   C. Reciting a poem
   D. Writing a thank you note

8. Of the following questions, which one would be most effective in helping ELLs learn to infer meaning? *(Average) (Skill 1.4)*

   A. How can we synthesize what you just said?
   B. What conclusions can you draw?
   C. What is the relationship between...?
   D. What evidence can you find...?

9. Asking students to make inferences increases learning in which domain? *(Average) (Skill 2.1)*

   A. Psychomotor
   B. Cognitive
   C. Affective
   D. Naturalistic

10. Which one of the scaffolding methods would be most effective in helping ELLs develop listing skills? *(Average) (Skill 2.2)*

    A. Frontloading vocabulary
    B. Asking ELLs to compare/contrast a listening activity with a text passage
    C. Listening several times
    D. Creating a word wall

11. When referring to a wealthy person as a "fat cat", the speaker is using a/an: *(Easy) (Skill 2.3)*

    A. cognate
    B. derivational morpheme
    C. phrase
    D. idiom

12. Which of the following theorists is associated with social interaction as an important facilitator of language learning? *(Average) (Skill 2.5)*

    A. Krashen
    B. Bernstein
    C. Vygotsky
    D. Hymes

13. Chomsky's Language Acquisition Device (LAD) includes all of the following hypotheses except: *(Average) (Skill 3.1)*

    A. language learners form hypotheses based on the language they receive
    B. enter the world as a blank slate
    C. test out hypotheses in speech and texts
    D. construct language

14. **Cummins stated children acquire BICS in approximately _____ years and CALPS in _____ years.**
    (Rigorous) (Skill 3.1)

    A. 3; 5-6
    B. 2; 5-7
    C. 4; 4-5
    D. 1; 3-5

15. **Language learners seem to acquire syntax:**
    (Easy) (Skill 3.2)

    A. at the same rate in L1 and L2
    B. faster in L2 than L1
    C. in the same order regardless of whether it is in L1 or L2
    D. in different order for L1

16. **The Schema Theory of Carrell & Eisterhold suggests that for learning to take place, teachers must:**
    (Rigorous) (Skill 3.3)

    A. integrate content areas with ESOL techniques
    B. emphasize all four language skills
    C. present comprehensible input in a meaningful context
    D. relate new materials to previous knowledge

17. **Abigail is an enthusiastic child who spontaneously cries when watching movies. She challenges the teacher in class, but is content to let her classmates make decisions. Which of the learning styles most accurately describes her?**
    (Rigorous) (Skill 3.3)

    A. Analytic
    B. Authority-oriented
    C. Communicative
    D. Concrete

18. **Young children are often considered better language learners than older children or adults. However, older children or adults may be able to progress more rapidly in reading instruction because:**
    (Rigorous) (Skill 3.3)

    A. they have more worldly experience to help them understand the texts
    B. their vocabulary concepts in L2 are less developed
    C. they have more language learning experience
    D. phonics is the same whether in L1 or L2

19. **The affective domain affects how students acquire a second language because:**
(Average) (Skill 3.4)

   A. learning a second language may make the learner feel vulnerable
   B. the attitude of peers and family is motivating
   C. motivation is a powerful personal factor
   D. facilitative anxiety determines our reaction to competition and is positive

20. **Interlanguage is best described as:**
(Easy) (Skill 3.4)

   A. a language characterized by overgeneralization
   B. bilingualism
   C. a language learning strategy
   D. a strategy characterized by poor grammar

21. **"The teacher 'writted' on the whiteboard" is an example of:**
(Easy) (Skill 3.4)

   A. simplification
   B. fossilization
   C. inter-language
   D. overgeneralization

22. **Simplification means:**
(Easy) (Skill 3.4)

   A. Adding 'ed' to irregular verbs as a way to use the past tense
   B. Stating 'I have a house beautiful in Miami' for 'I have a beautiful house in Miami'
   C. Hispanics pronouncing words like 'student' as 'estudent'
   D. Asking someone if 'You like?' instead of 'Do you like this one?

23. **In the statement "Peter, come here, please", the correct stress would be on:**
(Easy) (Skill 4.1)

   A. PEter; PLEASE
   B. peTER; HERE
   C. peTER: COME
   D. peTER; PLEASE

24. **"Bite" and "byte" are examples of which phonographemic differences?**
(Average) (Skill 4.1)

   A. Homonyms
   B. Homographs
   C. Homophones
   D. Heteronyms

25. **Words which have the same spelling or pronunciation, but different meanings are:**
   (Easy) (Skill 4.1)

   A. homonyms
   B. homographs
   C. homophones
   D. heteronyms

26. **If you are studying "morphemic analysis", then you are studying:**
   (Easy) (Skill 4.2)

   A. the smallest unit within a language system to which meaning is attached
   B. the root word and the suffix and/or prefix
   C. the way in which speech sounds form patterns
   D. answers A and B only

27. **The study of morphemes may provide the student with:**
   (Average) (Skill 2.2)

   A. the meaning of the root word
   B. the meaning of the phonemes
   C. grammatical information
   D. all of the above

28. **When the teacher is correcting a student's language, the teacher should:**
   (Easy) (Skill 4.2)

   A. carefully correct all mistakes
   B. consider the context of the error
   C. confirm the error by repeating it
   D. repeat the student's message but correct it

29. **If you are studying "syntax", then you are studying:**
   (Easy) (Skill 4.3)

   A. intonation and accent when conveying a message
   B. the rules for correct sentence structure
   C. the definition of individual words and meanings
   D. the subject-verb-object order of the English sentence

30. **In the following sentence: "Mary had few friends," which word is an example of a countable common noun?**
   (Easy) (Skill 4.3)

   A. Mary
   B. had
   C. few
   D. friends

31. To which subcategory of subordinating conjunction does "whether or not" belong?
(Average) (Skill 2.3)

   A. Time
   B. Cause and effect
   C. Contrast
   D. Condition

32. The sentence: "The bus was late and he was late, but John still managed to catch it." is an example of a

   _____ .
   (Rigorous) (Skill 2.3)

   A. simple sentence
   B. compound sentence
   C. complex sentence
   D. compound-complex sentence

33. Which one of the following is not a factor in people changing their register?
(Average) (Skill 3.1)

   A. The relationship between the speakers
   B. The formality of the situation
   C. The attitude towards the listeners and subject
   D. The culture of the speakers

34. Which of the following characteristics of textbook language makes it difficult for ELLs to understand?
(Rigorous) (Skill 4.3)

   A. Genre
   B. Passive voice
   C. Pronoun reference
   D. All of the above

35. Which one of the following is not included in the study of "semantics"?
(Rigorous) (Skill 4.4)

   A. Culture
   B. The definition of individual words and meanings
   C. The intonation of the speaker
   D. Meaning which is "stored" or "inherent", as well as "contextual"

36. If you are studying "pragmatics", then you are studying:
(Easy) (Skill 4.4)

   A. the definition of individual words and meanings
   B. how context impacts the interpretation of language
   C. meaning which is "stored" or "inherent", as well as "contextual"
   D. all of the above

37. **The theorist most associated with the study of dialects in the U.S. is _____ .**
(Average) (Skill 4.5)

A. Bernstein
B. Fishman
C. Hymes
D. Labov

38. **The term disglossia means _____ .**
(Average) (Skill 4.5)

A. use of language restricted to a limited close circle of speakers
B. speaking
C. use of separate dialects or use of separate language
D. a method of speaking when speakers do not share similar experiences or background

39. **Bernstein's research found that:**
(Rigorous) (Skill 4.5)

A. lower economic class children used the elaborated code
B. middle class children used the restricted code
C. middle class children used both the restricted code and the elaborated code
D. lower economic class children used both the restricted code and the elaborated code

40. **English has grown as a language primarily because of:**
(Easy) (Skill 3.1)

A. wars/technology and science
B. text messaging/immigrants
C. immigrants/technology and science
D. contemporary culture/wars

41. **Which of the following statements is true of the Ramirez Report?**
(Rigorous) (Skill 5.1)

A. Investigators believe that students' perceptions of a program are essential to the evaluation of a program's effectiveness.
B. The only hypothesized difference investigators found was the percentage of time teachers taught in English compared to Spanish in structured English Immersion Programs.
C. Teachers should reduce their English language demands when students are challenged cognitively, and vice versa.
D. There is a higher level of more serious demand than by those being educated for higher levels of competence in foreign language and second languages than usually occurs in school-based programs.

42. **Sheltered content teaching allows teachers to do all of the following except:**
(Rigorous) (Skill 5.3)

   A. use realia, word lists, gestures, etc.
   B. reduce language demands
   C. facilitate learning
   D. instruct in heritage language

43. **"Maria is a profesora" is an example of:**
(Rigorous) (Skill 4.3)

   A. dialect
   B. inter-language
   C. code-switching
   D. formulaic speech

44. **Which of the following activities encourages most the learning of new vocabulary?**
(Average) (Skill 6.1)

   A. Matching a vocabulary word with its definition
   B. Labeling classroom objects
   C. Singing
   D. Listening to a tape and recording pertinent information in a graphic organizer

45. **According to Ellis, two-way exchange of information shows more benefits in developing communication skills because:**
(Rigorous) (Skill 6.1)

   A. open-ended tasks have no correct response
   B. students enjoy chatting in class with peers
   C. students can anticipate outcomes better
   D. it requires more negotiation of meaning

46. **Which one of the following is not an activity used in developing speaking skills?**
(Rigorous) (Skill 6.1)

   A. Using manipulatives
   B. Interviews
   C. Structured interviews
   D. Role plays

47. **When teaching vocabulary to ELLs, all of the following are appropriate except:**
(Average) (Skill 6.1)

   A. describing a picture
   B. TPR
   C. Pictionary
   D. charades

48. **Informal assessment techniques include all of the following except:**
(Average) (Skill 6.2)

   A. oral interviews
   B. thumbs up/thumbs down
   C. end of course/term tests
   D. chapter quizzes

49. **The MELA-O evaluates ELLs:**
    (Rigorous) (Skill 6.2)

    A. who have a hearing disability
    B. proficiency in reading and writing
    C. proficiency in comprehension and production
    D. in a testing situation

50. **All of the following are characteristics of informal assessments except:**
    (Rigorous) (Skill 6.4)

    A. are performance based
    B. are required by the NCLB
    C. are used with scoring rubrics
    D. are continuous

51. **All of the following are characteristics of tests except:**
    (Rigorous) (Skill 6.4)

    A. compares a student's performance to grade level standards
    B. measures English proficiency more than construct for which they were designed
    C. determines a student's placement in special education classes
    D. may be influenced by ELLs from many different backgrounds

52. **When evaluating oral skills, which one of the following is an indication of a weakness?**
    (Easy) (Skill 6.4)

    A. Use of interjections and hesitations
    B. Intonation
    C. Vocabulary
    D. Fluency

53. **In a "bottom up" strategy of literacy development, which one of the following undesirable strategies might a reader use?**
    (Average) (Skill 7.1)

    A. Make guesses about what is going to happen
    B. Read all texts at the same speed
    C. Anticipate the contents of the text
    D. Infer meaning from sentences and paragraphs

54. **All of the following are important in developing literacy skills except:**
    (Average) (Skill 7.2)

    A. phonological awareness
    B. ability to sound out words
    C. fluency in word recognition
    D. syntax development

55. **In the cooperative learning task "jigsaw", students:**
    (Rigorous) (Skill 7.2)

    A. use open-ended questions
    B. pool meaning
    C. write headlines
    D. interview other students

56. ESOL instruction frequently requires the teacher to change his/her instruction methods. One of the most difficult may be the:
(Rigorous) (Skill 13.3)

A. wait time
B. establishment of group work
C. show and tell based on different cultures
D. extensive reading time

57. Which one of the following is not an effective instructional literacy practice?
(Rigorous) (Skill 7.2)

A. Providing direct explicit instruction of reading/writing skills based on ongoing student assessment
B. Devoting 40% of instructional time to reading/writing
C. Assessing student work based on common rubrics
D. Promoting conversation through purposeful and guided discussions about a book, piece of writing, or topic

58. Activities which focus on increasing fluency in academic reading include all of the following strategies except:
(Average) (Skill 7.3)

A. modeled reading
B. repeated reading of a familiar text
C. reading of signs, labels, and lists
D. coached reading of appropriate materials

59. Fluency is based upon all of the following except:
(Rigorous) (Skill 7.3)

A. a foundation of oral language skills
B. familiarity with letter forms
C. reading comprehension
D. efficient decoding skills

60. ESOL teaching encourages tasks that:
(Rigorous) (Skill 7.3)

A. emphasize correct form
B. give learners flexibility in problem solving
C. encourage learners to concentrate on language use
D. are demanding

61. **Which researcher is most associated with problem solving activities for language learning?**
(Rigorous) (Skill 7.3)

A. Gattegno
B. Prabhu
C. Wilkins
D. Lewis

62. **A purpose of the "reading phase" is to:**
(Rigorous) (Skill 7.4)

A. establish a purpose
B. utilize background knowledge to study heading, chapter, and answer questions
C. use graphics to organize information
D. motivate the reader

63. **When teaching initial literacy, teachers should focus on all of the following literacy skills except:**
(Average) (Skill 8.1)

A. culture
B. phonemic awareness
C. phonics
D. comprehension of different types of reading materials

64. **Which one of the following skills would probably have the most positive effect on developing literacy skills in ELLs?**
(Average) (Skill 8.2)

A. Oral storytelling traditions
B. Watching documentaries on TV
C. Visiting art museums
D. Attending concerts

65. **Which of the following is a disadvantage to the instructor's of use of L1 in the L2 classroom or in L2 instruction?**
(Rigorous) (Skill 8.2)

A. Limits development of L2
B. Reduces anxiety and fear
C. Permits explanation of differences and similarities of L1 and L2
D. Reduces time-consuming explanation of abstract concepts

66. **By acquiring knowledge of as few as _____ words, the ELL can understand _____ percent of an academic text.**
(Rigorous) (Skill 8.3)

A. 1000; 74
B. 1500; 80
C. 2000; 95
D. 2500; 60

67. **Which one of the following word analysis skills is probably the most difficult for an ELL to learn?**
(Average) (Skill 8.4)

A. Prefixes and suffixes
B. Sound-symbol correspondence
C. Phonemic and morphemic awareness
D. Cognates and false cognates

68. **Which of the following activities is the most effective in learning to use the dictionary effectively?**
(Rigorous) (Skill 8.4)

A. Locating synonyms, phrases, and etymology of words
B. Looking up definitions and writing a sentence with the words
C. Rewriting the definition in your own words
D. Writing down the pronunciation guide and the definition

69. **Incorporating prior knowledge into L2 learning does not:**
(Average) (Skill 8.4)

A. permit readers to learn and remember more
B. cause poor readers
C. help readers to evaluate new arguments
D. improve comprehension

70. **Which one of the following questions would be least effective in promoting critical-thinking skills when looking at a butterfly collection?**
(Rigorous) (Skill 8.4)

A. What are the parts of a butterfly?
B. What evidence do you find to support the idea...?
C. How would you classify a butterfly?
D. What colors are the butterflies?

71. **Which of the following is a meta-cognitive strategy?**
(Average) (Skill 8.4)

A. Practicing new language
B. Summarizing long passages
C. Skimming for necessary information
D. Evaluating learning

72. **To analyze oral discourse, which of the following is not an analytical question?**
(Rigorous) (Skill 8.4)

A. How did you feel about the dialogue?
B. How would you restate what the speaker said?
C. How would people from your country act in a similar situation?
D. Do you agree or disagree with what is said in the dialogue?

73. **Which one of the following is not a purpose of informal reading assessment?**
(Easy) (Skill 8.5)

A. To gauge oral reading comprehension
B. To assess vocabulary
C. To assess fluency
D. To assess silent reading comprehension

74. **Which one of the following is not a way to establish reliability when placing students with disabilities?**
(Easy) (Skill 8.6)

A. Using multiple raters
B. Including multiple assessment measures
C. Establishing clearly specified scoring criteria
D. Using the Woodcock-Johnson III Diagnostic Reading Battery

75. **Which of the following is not a step in the Language Experience Approach?**
(Average) (Skill 6.1)

A. Students draw a picture to represent something personal about an experience
B. Students dictate their story to the teacher
C. The teacher reads the story revising where necessary
D. The story is read in later days as a follow-up activity

76. **Which one of the following is not a way to encourage non-graded writing practice?**
(Easy) (Skill 9.1)

A. Writing a dialog in pairs
B. Rewriting a passage or summary in the ELL's own words
C. Writing from the perspective of another
D. Writing a summary to hand in

77. **The purpose of frontloading vocabulary is:**
(Average) (Skill 9.1)

A. vocabulary development
B. increase reading comprehension
C. explaining content
D. increasing spelling proficiency

78. **Reid (1987) divides the writing process into two broad divisions. They are:**
(Average) (Skill 9.2)

A. composing; pre-writing
B. pre-writing; drafting
C. brainstorming; drafting
D. composition; revision

79. Which one of the following writing activities is not appropriate for different proficiency levels?
(Average) (Skill 9.3)

A. Reading and writing letters to pen pals
B. Creating exhibits or projects
C. Traditional book reports
D. Organizing lists

80. Which one of the following is not an appropriate activity for engaging ELLs in real-life communicative activities?
(Average) (Skill 9.3)

A. Oral discussion based on a news story
B. Researching an assigned topic and reporting back to peers
C. Reporting on a new video game
D. Discussing a movie with a friend

81. Emerging ELLs need instruction in conventions of written Standard English such as:
(Average) (Skill 9.4)

A. syntax
B. discourse
C. vocabulary
D. types of written texts

82. Which one of the following is not a valid purpose of assessment?
(Rigorous) (Skill 9.5)

A. Determining a student's potential
B. Determination of a student's present academic performance level
C. Eligibility for a program
D. Diagnosis of special learner disabilities

83. Tests which evaluate an individual as compared to others are:
(Easy) (Skill 9.5)

A. standardized
B. authentic
C. norm referenced
D. criterion referenced

84. Which of the following tests is used to refine specific learning disabilities?
(Rigorous) (Skill 9.5)

A. Wechsler Intelligence Scale for Children
B. Sanford-Binet IV
C. Gardner's multiple intelligence tests
D. Kaufman Assessment Batter for Children

85. **Which one of the following goals will not be discovered through assessment?**
(Rigorous) (Skill 9.5)

    A. If student is ready for new information
    B. Strategies for improving programs
    C. If student is lacking prerequisite skills
    D. Program weaknesses

86. **Which of the following writing assessments uses holistic scoring?**
(Rigorous) (Skill 9.5)

    A. International English Language Test System (IELTS)
    B. National Assessment of Educational Progress (NAEP)
    C. Test of English as a Foreign Language (TOEFL)
    D. Michigan Writing Assessment

87. **Which one of the following is a disadvantage of portfolio assessment?**
(Average) (Skill 9.5)

    A. They are integrative
    B. They produce variable samples
    C. They are motivating
    D. They are formative

88. **Arreaga-Mayer (1998) suggests all of the following constructs for successful ELLs except:**
(Rigorous) (Skill 10.1)

    A. collaborative/cooperative learning
    B. input slightly above competence level
    C. involvement
    D. mediation/feedback

89. **Which one of the following is not one of the four basic components of peer tutoring?**
(Average) (Skill 10.1)

    A. Weekly competing teams
    B. Highly structured teaching procedures
    C. Daily, public postings of individual and team scores
    D. Building on prior knowledge

90. **All of the following are integrated approaches to language teaching except:**
(Average) (Skill 10.1)

    A. Language Experience Approach
    B. cooperative learning
    C. task-based or experiential learning
    D. graphic organizers

91. **Graphic organizers provide students with:**
(Average) (Skill 10.1)

A. projects to carry out
B. a means for organizing information
C. negotiated meaning
D. cooperative incentivizes

92. **According to Chomsky's Universal Grammar (UG) and Language Acquisition Device (LAD) theories, younger learners have less difficulty learning language because:**
(Rigorous) (Skill 10.3)

A. language is controlled by external factors
B. after puberty, the critical period shuts down
C. their LAD is still active
D. language abilities increase with age

93. **All of the following are advantages of learning and using more than one language except:**
(Rigorous) (Skill 10. 3)

A. increases visual-social abilities
B. supports cognitive flexibility
C. limits problem solving abilities
D. allows increased understanding of concepts

94. **All of the following are true about the Massachusetts Comprehensive Assessment System (MCAS) except:**
(Rigorous) (Skill 10.4)

A. Each public school student in the state is tested in grades 3-8 and once in high school in English.
B. The Massachusetts Curriculum Frameworks forms the basis of the test battery.
C. Each public school student in the state is tested in grades 3-8 and once in high school in mathematics.
D. Each public school student in the state is tested in grades 3-8 and once in high school in computer science.

95. **To distinguish between ELLs and ELLs with disabilities, which one of the following testing procedures is not recommended?**
(Average) (Skill 10.4)

A. Intelligence quotient (IQ) test
B. Criterion-referenced assessments
C. Curriculum-referenced assessments
D. Observations from school, home, and community

96. When considering students with behavioral disabilities, teachers are most concerned about behaviors which are:
(Rigorous) (Skill 10.4)

A. sporadic
B. intense
C. short-lived
D. infrequent

97. Teacher Assistance Teams (TATS) should be composed of all of the following except the:
(Average) (Skill 10.4)

A. school administrators
B. guidance counselors
C. media specialists
D. parent(s)

98. When considering referrals for specialized services, all of the following are considered except:
(Rigorous) (Skill 10.4)

A. student characteristics
B. parents' request for/against referral
C. multidisciplinary evaluation
D. institutional factors

99. To protect students from inequities in the referral process, federal law explicitly provides for:
(Rigorous) (Skill 10.4)

A. non-discriminatory evaluation procedures
B. an independent education evaluation
C. a multidisciplinary team using several pieces of information to formulate a referral
D. testing of the child in L1 unless clearly not feasible to do so

100. Information for placing students with learning or behavioral disabilities will usually include all of the following except:
(Rigorous) (Skill 10.4)

A. past academic performance
B. neurological reports
C. notes from auxiliary/substitute teachers
D. speech and language evaluations

RIGOR TABLE

EASY	7, 11, 15, 20, 21, 22, 23, 25, 26, 28, 29, 30, 36, 40, 52, 73, 74, 76, 83
AVERAGE	1, 3, 4, 5, 6, 8, 9, 10, 12, 13, 19, 24, 27, 31, 33, 37, 38, 44, 47, 48, 53, 54, 58, 63, 64, 67, 69, 71, 75, 77, 78, 79, 80, 81, 87, 89, 90, 91, 95, 97
RIGOROUS	2, 14, 16, 17, 18, 32, 34, 35, 39, 41, 42, 43, 45, 46, 49, 50, 51, 55, 56, 57, 59, 60, 61, 62, 65, 66, 68, 70, 72, 82, 84, 85, 86, 88, 92, 93, 94, 96, 98, 99, 100

ANSWER KEY

1. C	46. A	91. B
2. C	47. A	92. C
3. D	48. C	93. C
4. A	49. C	94. D
5. B	50. B	95. A
6. C	51. C	96. B
7. A	52. A	97. C
8. D	53. B	98. C
9. B	54. D	99. B
10. C	55. B	100. C
11. D	56. A	
12. C	57. B	
13. B	58. C	
14. B	59. C	
15. C	60. B	
16. D	61. B	
17. D	62. B	
18. A	63. A	
19. A	64. A	
20. C	65. A	
21. D	66. C	
22. D	67. B	
23. A	68. A	
24. C	69. B	
25. B	70. D	
26. D	71. D	
27. C	72. B	
28. D	73. C	
29. B	74. D	
30. D	75. C	
31. D	76. D	
32. B	77. B	
33. D	78. D	
34. D	79. C	
35. A	80. B	
36. B	81. A	
37. D	82. A	
38. C	83. C	
39. C	84. C	
40. C	85. B	
41. B	86. C	
42. D	87. B	
43. C	88. B	
44. C	89. D	
45. D	90. A	

Sample Test with Rationales

1. **ELLs who are practicing listening skills might be asked to:**
   (Average) (Skill 1.1)

   A. record their voice
   B. listen to the TV
   C. summarize a listening selection in a journal
   D. audio tape a passage from a TV program, radio, or native speaker

Answer: C. summarize a listening selection in a journal
Answers B and D suggest the ELL actively engage in listening activities. However, there is no follow-up to demonstrate active listening took place. These options may be discarded. Answer A has little value unless the ELL listens to the recording for specific mistakes in grammar, pronunciation, or intonation. The best option is C where the ELL is listening and then writing a summary (criticism, opinion, etc.) of what was heard.

2. **An effective way to teach students to actively listen for information would be:**
   (Rigorous) (Skill 1.2)

   A. asking comprehension questions after completing a listening activity
   B. frontloading vocabulary
   C. provide a graphic organizer to be filled in during the listening activity
   D. quiz

Answer: C. provide a graphic organizer to be filled in during the listening activity
Answer A is ineffective because students will frequently "tune out" of listening activities because they don't understand and listening is hard work. Answer B is effective for helping the ELL to understand what he/she is going to hear. Answer D is the least effective option because it may raise anxiety levels and block learning. ELLs need to be trained to listen during the entire passage by actively engaging with the passage. Answer C is the best choice.

3. **Students need to monitor their listening strategies because:**
    (Average) (Skill 1.2)

    A. monitoring is an ineffective learning strategy
    B. the ELL needs to work on self-improvement strategies
    C. monitoring listening activities helps ELLs see their mistakes
    D. not all strategies are effective

Answer: D. not all strategies are effective
Answer A may be discarded since monitoring is a very effective learning strategy. Answer B might be indicative of a learner who needs help in determining effective learning strategies and reasonable goals. Answer C suggests that through monitoring ELLS will learn what listening mistakes they are having. Monitoring listening strategies will not help with this goal. The best option is D. An ELL needs to monitor his/her strategies to determine which listening strategies are effective and which others might be needed.

4. **All of the following are reasons an ELL will not respond in a listening class except:**
    (Average) (Skill 1.3)

    A. feels the class is a waste of his/her time
    B. has nothing to say
    C. doesn't know what to say
    D. is embarrassed to admit they didn't understand

Answer: A. feels the class is a waste of his/her time
Answers B, C, and D are common reasons for an ELL not to respond or participate in a listening class. The occasional ELL may feel that he/she already knows enough English to adequately respond and can't wait to be released from the ESOL class. This reaction is rare, but possible if accurate placement is not obtained. Answer A is the best choice.

5. **A major factor in reluctance to speak in language class is:**
    (Average) (Skill 1.3)

    A. voice
    B. anxiety
    C. gestures
    D. mime

Answer: B. anxiety
Answers A, C, and D are all methods of communicating in an ESOL class. Answer B refers to a debilitating condition which inhibits communication. B is the best choice.

6.   **All of the following are examples of BICS except:**
     (Average) (Skill 1.3)

     A. Call me.
     B. Text me after the game.
     C. Work on problems 1-5.
     D. Please give me a fruit salad and a glass of milk.

Answer: C. Work on problems 1-5.
Answers A, B, and D are Basic Interpersonal Communication Skills (BICS). Answer C is a Cognitive Academic Language Proficiency (CALP) skill.

7.   **Which one of the following activities encourages paraphrasing skills?**
     (Easy) (Skill 1.4)

     A. Condensing a paragraph
     B. Explaining a math problem
     C. Reciting a poem
     D. Writing a thank you note

Answer: A. Condensing a paragraph
Answers B, C, and D are excellent ESOL activities, but do not encourage rephrasing of a message in one's own words of a message that has been read or heard. Only Answer A involves repeating a message in a different way.

8.   **Of the following questions, which one would be most effective in helping ELLs learn to infer meaning?**
     (Average) (Skill 1.4)

     A. How can we synthesize what you just said?
     B. What conclusions can you draw?
     C. What is the relationship between...?
     D. What evidence can you find...?

Answer: D. What evidence can you find...?
Answer A is a paraphrasing technique. Both Answers B and C refer to drawing conclusions. Only Answer D asks the student to support meaning which is inferred.

9. **Asking students to make inferences increases learning in which domain?**
(Average) (Skill 2.1)

A. Psychomotor
B. Cognitive
C. Affective
D. Naturalistic

Answer: B. Cognitive
Answer A deals with motor skills, communication and creating. Answer C concerns feelings, attitudes, and values. Answer D may be dismissed as this is one of the eight multiple intelligences of Gardner. Answer B is the domain where mental operations occur.

10. **Which one of the scaffolding methods would be most effective in helping ELLs develop listing skills?**
(Average) (Skill 2.2)

A. Frontloading vocabulary
B. Asking ELLs to compare/contrast a listening activity with a text passage
C. Listening several times
D. Creating a word wall

Answer: C. Listening several times
While all of the answers are effective scaffolding techniques, until understanding is achieved, learning does not occur. The best option would be C, allowing the ELL to listen several times.

11. **When referring to a wealthy person as a "fat cat", the speaker is using a/an:**
(Easy) (Skill 2.3)

A. cognate
B. derivational morpheme
C. phrase
D. idiom

Answer: D. idiom
Idioms are new meanings assigned to words that already have a meaning in a language. The expression 'fat cat' literally means a cat that is fat. However, it has become an idiomatic way to say someone is a wealthy person.

12. **Which of the following theorists is associated with social interaction as an important facilitator of language learning?**
    (Average) (Skill 2.5)

    A. Krashen
    B. Bernstein
    C. Vygotsky
    D. Hymes

Answer: C. Vygotsky
Answer A Krashen formulated The Monitor Model. Answer B Bernstein researched restricted and elaborated codes. Answer D Hymes theorized on communicative competence. Answer C Vygotsky theorized on the importance of social interaction in the language learning process.

13. **Chomsky's Language Acquisition Device (LAD) includes all of the following hypotheses except:**
    (Average) (Skill 3.1)

    A. language learners form hypotheses based on the language they receive
    B. enter the world as a blank slate
    C. test out hypotheses in speech and texts
    D. construct language

Answer: B. enter the world as a blank slate
The essence of Chomsky's theory is that children do not enter the world as a blank slate, but rather have a LAD which permits the construction of their language regardless of which language it may be. The LAD is innate. Therefore, Option B is the correct choice as it does not support Chomsky's theory.

14. **Cummins stated children acquire BICS in approximately _____ years and CALPS in _____ years.**
    (Rigorous) (Skill 3.1)

    A. 3; 5-6
    B. 2; 5-7
    C. 4; 4-5
    D. 1; 3-5

Answer: B. 2; 5-7
The correct option is B.

15.   **Language learners seem to acquire syntax:**
      (Easy) (Skill 3.2)

      A. at the same rate in L1 and L2
      B. faster in L2 than L1
      C. in the same order regardless of whether it is in L1 or L2
      D. in different order for L1

Answer: C. in the same order regardless of whether it is in L1 or L2
All language learners must progress through the same hierarchical steps in their language learning process. They go from the least to the most complicated stages regardless of whether it is in the L1 or L2.

16.   **The Schema Theory of Carrell & Eisterhold suggests that for learning to take place, teachers must:**
      (Rigorous) (Skill 3.3)

      A. integrate content areas with ESOL techniques
      B. emphasize all four language skills
      C. present comprehensible input in a meaningful context
      D. relate new materials to previous knowledge

Answer: D. relate new materials to previous knowledge
The schema theory of Carrell & Eisterhold suggests that schema must be related to previous knowledge or learning does not take place. When activated, schema are able to evaluate the new materials in light of previous knowledge. If the arguments are made convincing to the learner, he or she accepts them and integrates the new knowledge in to his/her data bank. Otherwise, the new materials are unconvincing, and the new knowledge is rejected by the learner.

17. Abigail is an enthusiastic child who spontaneously cries when watching movies. She challenges the teacher in class, but is content to let her classmates make decisions. Which of the learning styles most accurately describes her?
(Rigorous) (Skill 3.3)

   A. Analytic
   B. Authority-oriented
   C. Communicative
   D. Concrete

Answer: D. Concrete

Analytic (A) learning style students are object oriented, so this option may be discarded. An authority-oriented (B) learning style student would not challenge the teacher, and so Option B may be discarded. A communicative (C) learning style student likes making decisions and social learning situations. Abigail does not like making decisions, so Option C can be eliminated. The best choice is D Concrete learning style where the learner is people-oriented, emotional, and spontaneous.

18. Young children are often considered better language learners than older children or adults. However, older children or adults may be able to progress more rapidly in reading instruction because:
(Rigorous) (Skill 3.3)

   A. they have more worldly experience to help them understand the texts
   B. their vocabulary concepts in L2 are less developed
   C. they have more language learning experience
   D. phonics is the same whether in L1 or L2

Answer: A. they have more worldly experience to help them understand the texts

Answers B and C would depend on the individuals involved in the learning situation. Answer D can readily be discarded as sounds are what distinguish many languages one from another. The correct answer is A. Older learners can apply their worldly experience and schema developed in L1 to understanding L2 texts as well as other language learning situations.

19. **The affective domain affects how students acquire a second language because:**
(Average) (Skill 3.4)

A. learning a second language may make the learner feel vulnerable
B. the attitude of peers and family is motivating
C. motivation is a powerful personal factor
D. facilitative anxiety determines our reaction to competition and is positive

Answer: A. learning a second language may make the learner feel vulnerable
The affective domain refers to the full range of human feelings and emotions that come into play during second language acquisition. Learning a second language may make the learner vulnerable because they may have to leave their comfort zone behind. This can be especially difficult for adults who are used to being 'powerful' or 'in control' in their profession, but also affects children and teens. Option A is the best selection.

20. **Interlanguage is best described as:**
(Easy) (Skill 3.4)

A. a language characterized by overgeneralization
B. bilingualism
C. a language learning strategy
D. a strategy characterized by poor grammar

Answer: C. a language learning strategy
Interlanguage occurs when the second language learner lacks proficiency in L2 and tries to compensate for his or her lack of fluency in the new language. Three components are overgeneralization, simplification, and L1 interference or language transfer. Therefore, answer A is only one component of interlanguage making option C the correct answer.

21. **"The teacher 'writted' on the whiteboard" is an example of:**
(Easy) (Skill 3.4)

A. simplification
B. fossilization
C. inter-language
D. overgeneralization

Answer: D. overgeneralization
In this case, the ELL has tried to apply the rule of /ed/ endings to an irregular verb to form the past tense verb, i.e., he has used 'overgeneralization' to create an incorrect verb form. The correct answer is D.

22.   **Simplification means:**
       (Easy) (Skill 3.4)

    A. Adding 'ed' to irregular verbs as a way to use the past tense
    B. Stating 'I have a house beautiful in Miami' for 'I have a beautiful house in Miami'
    C. Hispanics pronouncing words like 'student' as 'estudent'
    D. Asking someone if 'You like?' instead of 'Do you like this one?'

Answer: D. Asking someone if 'You like?' instead of 'Do you like this one?'
Simplification is a common learner error involving simplifying the language where the correct structures have not been internalized. In this case, the correct question form has not been acquired though the ELLs meaning is clear.

23.   **In the statement "Peter, come here, please", the correct stress would be on:**
       (Easy) (Skill 4.1)

    A. PEter; PLEASE
    B. peTER; HERE
    C. peTER: COME
    D. peTER; PLEASE

Answer: A. PEter; PLEASE
Answer A reflects normal stress in this statement.

24.   **"Bite" and "byte' are examples of which phonographemic differences?**
       (Average) (Skill 4.1)

    A. Homonyms
    B. Homographs
    C. Homophones
    D. Heteronyms

Answer: C. Homophones
'Homonyms' is a general term for words with two or more meanings. Homographs are two or more words with the same spelling or pronunciation, but different meanings. Heteronyms are two or more words that have the same spelling but different meanings and spellings. Homophones are words that have the same pronunciation, but different meanings and spellings. C is the correct response.

25. **Words which have the same spelling or pronunciation, but different meanings are:**
    (Easy) (Skill 4.1)

    A. homonyms
    B. homographs
    C. homophones
    D. heteronyms

Answer: B. homographs
See explanation given after question 24.

26. **If you are studying "morphemic analysis", then you are studying:**
    (Easy) (Skill 4.2)

    A. the smallest unit within a language system to which meaning is attached
    B. the root word and the suffix and/or prefix
    C. the way in which speech sounds form patterns
    D. answers A and B only

Answer: D. answers A and B only
The study of the way in which speech sounds form patterns is called phonology. The smallest unit within a language system to which meaning is attached is a morpheme. The root word and the suffix and/or prefix are components of morphemes and basic to the analysis of a word. Therefore, both A and B are necessary for the study of morphemic analysis so the correct answer is D.

27. **The study of morphemes may provide the student with:**
    (Average) (Skill 2.2)

    A. the meaning of the root word
    B. the meaning of the phonemes
    C. grammatical information
    D. all of the above

Answer: C. grammatical information
The meaning of the root word comes from its source or origin, and the meaning of phonemes relates to its sound. The correct answer is C. Grammatical morphemes give information to show how the parts of a sentence relate to each other (e.g. prepositions or articles).

28. **When the teacher is correcting a student's language, the teacher should:**
     (Easy) (Skill 4.2)

     A. carefully correct all mistakes
     B. consider the context of the error
     C. confirm the error by repeating it
     D. repeat the student's message but correct it

Answer: D. repeat the student's message but correct it

To carefully correct all mistakes a student makes would raise the affective filter and probably cause the student to hesitate before speaking. Considering the context of the error gives the teacher insight into the student's learning, but isn't a method of correction. To confirm the error by repeating it would suggest to the student that his or her utterance was correct and is not good practice. The best option is D which corrects the error but in a way that shows the student the correct form without embarrassing him or her.

29. **If you are studying "syntax", then you are studying:**
     (Easy) (Skill 4.3)

     A. intonation and accent when conveying a message
     B. the rules for correct sentence structure
     C. the definition of individual words and meanings
     D. the subject-verb-object order of the English sentence

Answer: B. the rules for correct sentence structure

The intonation and accent used when conveying a message refer to pitch and stress. The definition of individual words and meanings is semantics. The subject-verb-object order of the English sentence refers to is the correct order for most English sentences, but the rules for correct sentence structure refers to syntax, so B is the best option.

30. **In the following sentence: "Mary had few friends," which word is an example of a countable common noun?**
     (Easy) (Skill 4.3)

     A. Mary
     B. had
     C. few
     D. friends

Answer: D. friends

Option A is incorrect as Mary is a countable proper noun. Option B is a verb. Option C is used when referring to countable nouns but is an adjective. Option D is the correct choice since one's friends may be counted.

31. **To which subcategory of subordinating conjunction does "whether or not" belong?**
    (Average) (Skill 2.3)

    A. Time
    B. Cause and effect
    C. Contrast
    D. Condition

Answer: D. Condition
Time conjunctions (Option A) are those referring to time, such as: after, before, while, etc. Option B, cause and effect conjunctions, includes because, now that, since, etc. Option C, refers to conjunctions such as although, even though, thought, etc. Condition conjunctions (Option D) include if, unless, whether or not, etc. Option D is the correct choice.

32. **The sentence: "The bus was late and he was late, but John still managed to catch it." is an example of a _____ .**
    (Rigorous) (Skill 2.3)

    A. simple sentence
    B. compound sentence
    C. complex sentence
    D. compound-complex sentence

Answer: B. compound sentence
Answer A may be eliminated since the sentence contains three independent clauses. Since there are no independent clauses, Answer C and D may be eliminated. Thus, Answer B is the correct choice.

33. **Which one of the following is not a factor in people changing their register?**
    (Average) (Skill 3.1)

    A. The relationship between the speakers
    B. The formality of the situation
    C. The attitude towards the listeners and subject
    D. The culture of the speakers

Answer: D. The culture of the speakers
People change their register depending on the relationship between the speakers, the formality of the situation, and the attitudes towards the listeners and the subject. Answer D—culture of the speakers—is not a reason for people to change their register.

34. **Which of the following characteristics of textbook language makes it difficult for ELLs to understand?**
(Rigorous) (Skill 4.3)

    A. Genre
    B. Passive voice
    C. Pronoun reference
    D. All of the above

Answer: D. All of the above
Answer A: each genre has a distinct organizational pattern and writing style. Answer B: The passive voice is common in textbooks, especially science textbooks. Answer C: To whom or what a pronoun refers can be obscure and cause problems for ELLs, too. Thus, D is the correct choice. Textbook language is difficult for most ELLs for many different reasons.

35. **Which one of the following is not included in the study of "semantics"?**
(Rigorous) (Skill 4.4)

    A. Culture
    B. The definition of individual words and meanings
    C. The intonation of the speaker
    D. Meaning which is "stored" or "inherent", as well as "contextual"

Answer: A. Culture
Since semantics refers to the definition of individual words and meanings, the intonation of the speaker, and meaning which is "stored" or "inherent", as well as "contextual", option A is the best response.

36. **If you are studying "pragmatics", then you are studying:**
(Easy) (Skill 4.4)

    A. the definition of individual words and meanings
    B. how context impacts the interpretation of language
    C. meaning which is "stored" or "inherent", as well as "contextual"
    D. all of the above

Answer: B. how context impacts the interpretation of language
The definition of individual words and meanings refers to semantics. Meaning which is "stored" or "inherent", as well as "contextual" refers to the lexicon of a language. The best option is B as pragmatics refers to studies of how context impacts the interpretation of language.

37. **The theorist most associated with the study of dialects in the U.S. is _____.**
    (Average) (Skill 4.5)

    A. Bernstein
    B. Fishman
    C. Hymes
    D. Labov

Answer: D. Labov
Answer A: Bernstein theorized about restricted and elaborated codes. Answer B: Fishman studied disglossia. Answer C: Hymes worked on communicative competence in ELLs. Answer D: Labov researched the African-American dialect and is the correct choice.

38. **The term disglossia means _____.**
    (Average) (Skill 4.5)

    A. use of language restricted to a limited close circle of speakers
    B. speaking
    C. use of separate dialects or use of separate language
    D. a method of speaking when speakers do not share similar experiences or background

Answer: C. use of separate dialects or use of separate language
Answer A refers to Bernstein's restricted code and D to his elaborated code. Answer B is an acronym Hymes devised to explain the abilities of a native speaker. Answer C is a definition of disglossia and the correct choice.

39. **Bernstein's research found that:**
    (Rigorous) (Skill 4.5)

    A. lower economic class children used the elaborated code
    B. middle class children used the restricted code
    C. middle class children used both the restricted code and the elaborated code
    D. lower economic class children used both the restricted code and the elaborated code

Answer: C. middle class children used both the restricted code and the elaborated code
Bernstein's studies showed that lower socio-economic status children used only the restricted code while middle class children showed greater ability to use both codes. Answer C is the correct choice.

40. **English has grown as a language primarily because of:**
    (Easy) (Skill 3.1)

    A. wars/technology and science
    B. text messaging/immigrants
    C. immigrants/technology and science
    D. contemporary culture/wars

Answer: C. immigrants/technology and science
While all of the options have influenced the growth of English, new immigrants continually adding new words to the language is the most influential factor. The second largest body of new words comes from technology and science making Option C the best option.

41. **Which of the following statements is true of the Ramirez Report?**
    (Rigorous) (Skill 5.1)

    A. Investigators believe that students' perceptions of a program are essential to the evaluation of a program's effectiveness.
    B. The only hypothesized difference investigators found was the percentage of time teachers taught in English compared to Spanish in structured English Immersion Programs.
    C. Teachers should reduce their English language demands when students are challenged cognitively, and vice versa.
    D. There is a higher level of more serious demand than by those being educated for higher levels of competence in foreign language and second languages than usually occurs in school-based programs.

Answer: B. The only hypothesized difference investigators found was the percentage of time teachers taught in English compared to Spanish in structured English Immersion Programs.
Answer A refers to the Amigos Program reported on by Cabazon, Lambert & Hall, 1992. Answer C refers to statements of Gersten and Baker, 2001. Answer D is a distinction discovered by Lambert, 1990. Answer B is the correct one since it was a conclusion of the U.S. Department of Education, 1991, and informally known as the Ramirez Report.

42. **Sheltered content teaching allows teachers to do all of the following except:**
(Rigorous) (Skill 5.3)

A. use realia, word lists, gestures, etc.
B. reduce language demands
C. facilitate learning
D. instruct in heritage language

Answer: D. instruct in heritage language
Answers A, B, and C are all part of Shelter Content Teaching strategies. Answer D is not an element of this strategy and is the correct choice.

43. **"Maria is a profesora" is an example of:**
(Rigorous) (Skill 4.3)

A. dialect
B. inter-language
C. code-switching
D. formulaic speech

Answer: C. code-switching
Dialect is any form or variety of a spoken language peculiar to a region, community, social group, etc. Inter-language is the language spoken by ELLs that is between their L1 and L2. Formulaic speech refers to speech that is ritualistic in nature and perhaps used for social politeness rather than information.

Sociolinguistics is a very broad term used to understand the relationship between language and people including the phenomenon of people switching languages during a conversation. One person may switch languages when a word is not known in the other language. Option C is the correct option.

44. **Which of the following activities encourages most the learning of new vocabulary?**
    (Average) (Skill 6.1)

    A. Matching a vocabulary word with its definition
    B. Labeling classroom objects
    C. Singing
    D. Listening to a tape and recording pertinent information in a graphic organizer

Answer: C. Singing
Both Answers A and B are passive activities which do not require the learner to use the language. Answer D is an effective listening strategy, but the learner is trying to understand and remember the material, not learn vocabulary. Only Answer C facilitates the learning of language and/or vocabulary.

45. **According to Ellis, two-way exchange of information shows more benefits in developing communication skills because:**
    (Rigorous) (Skill 6.1)

    A. open-ended tasks have no correct response
    B. students enjoy chatting in class with peers
    C. students can anticipate outcomes better
    D. it requires more negotiation of meaning

Answer: D. it requires more negotiation of meaning
Only Answer D was a conclusion of Ellis' study.

46. **Which one of the following is not an activity used in developing speaking skills?**
    (Rigorous) (Skill 6.1)

    A. Using manipulatives
    B. Interviews
    C. Structured interviews
    D. Role plays

Answer: A. Using manipulatives
Answers B, C, and D are all effective strategies for developing speaking skills. The use of manipulatives is an instructional method of teachers to convey meaning. Answer A is the correct choice.

47.   When teaching vocabulary to ELLs, all of the following are appropriate except:
      (Average) (Skill 6.1)

      A. describing a picture
      B. TPR
      C. Pictionary
      D. charades

Answer: A. describing a picture
Answers B, C, and D are all appropriate vocabulary development activities which can be adjusted to the age of the students. Answer A is an exercise for demonstrating previously learned vocabulary, but anxiety produced by the activity (in some learners) would probably negate any active learning.

48.   Informal assessment techniques include all of the following except:
      (Average) (Skill 6.2)

      A. oral interviews
      B. thumbs up/thumbs down
      C. end of course/term tests
      D. chapter quizzes

Answer: C. end of course/term tests
All options are assessments. Only Answer C is considered a formal assessment.

49.   The MELA-O evaluates ELLs:
      (Rigorous) (Skill 6.2)

      A. who have a hearing disability
      B. proficiency in reading and writing
      C. proficiency in comprehension and production
      D. in a testing situation

Answer: C. proficiency in comprehension and production
Answer A may be discarded since in Massachusetts all LEP (more recently ELLs) students are required to take the MELA-O unless a hearing disability is noted on the IEP. Answer B may be discarded as the MELA-R/W tests ELLs in these areas. Answer D may be discarded as the MELA-O evaluates ELLs in a classroom setting while students engage in interactive academic activities. Only Answer C is correct. Proficiency in comprehension and production are the components evaluated by the MELA-O.

50. All of the following are characteristics of informal assessments except: *(Rigorous) (Skill 6.4)*

   A. are performance based
   B. are required by the NCLB
   C. are used with scoring rubrics
   D. are continuous

Answer: B. are required by the NCLB
Only Answer B is correct since the NCLB Act makes no mention of informal assessments.

51. All of the following are characteristics of tests except: *(Rigorous) (Skill 6.4)*

   A. compares a student's performance to grade level standards
   B. measures English proficiency more than construct for which they were designed
   C. determines a student's placement in special education classes
   D. may be influenced by ELLs from many different backgrounds

Answer: C. determines a student's placement in special education classes
According to research, Answers A, B, and D are all characteristics of tests. Only Answer C is inaccurate as many factors, as well as different types of reports and records, lead up to placement in special education classes, not just tests.

52. When evaluating oral skills, which one of the following is an indication of a weakness? *(Easy) (Skill 6.4)*

   A. Use of interjections and hesitations
   B. Intonation
   C. Vocabulary
   D. Fluency

Answer: A. Use of interjections and hesitations
Answers B, C, and D may either be good or poor. Only Answer A is a clear weakness, and therefore, the correct answer.

53.   In a "bottom up" strategy of literacy development, which one of the following undesirable strategies might a reader use?
(Average) (Skill 7.1)

A. Make guesses about what is going to happen
B. Read all texts at the same speed
C. Anticipate the contents of the text
D. Infer meaning from sentences and paragraphs

Answer: B. Read all texts at the same speed
Options A, C, and D are all advantages of a "top down" strategy and are desirable reading strategies. Only Option B is undesirable and the correct answer.

54.   All of the following are important in developing literacy skills except:
(Average) (Skill 7.2)

A. phonological awareness
B. ability to sound out words
C. fluency in word recognition
D. syntax development

Answer: D. syntax development
Answers A, B, and C are all skills to development literacy. The correct answer is D.

55.   In the cooperative learning task "jigsaw", students:
(Rigorous) (Skill 7.2)

A. use open-ended questions
B. pool meaning
C. write headlines
D. interview other students

Answer: B. pool meaning
Answer A is utilized in many cooperative learning activities including Information Gap Activities. Answer C, writing headlines, is a way to summarize information. Answer D, interviewing other students, is another Communicative Language Activity. A characteristic of "jigsaw" is that students pool their information in order to fully understand a text. Answer B is the correct choice.

56. **ESOL instruction frequently requires the teacher to change his/her instruction methods. One of the most difficult may be the:**
(Rigorous) (Skill 13.3)

   A. wait time
   B. establishment of group work
   C. show and tell based on different cultures
   D. extensive reading time

Answer: A. wait time
Answer B, C, and D can all be discounted since they are standard practice for language arts teachers. Answer A, the amount of time a teacher waits for an answer from students, can be very difficult to change. Teachers may be somewhat impatient ('Let's get on with it'), lack understanding ('If they knew the answer, they would respond'), and unaware of differences between the U.S. and other cultures. Answer A is the correct response.

57. **Which one of the following is not an effective instructional literacy practice?**
(Rigorous) (Skill 7.2)

   A. Providing direct explicit instruction of reading/writing skills based on ongoing student assessment
   B. Devoting 40% of instructional time to reading/writing
   C. Assessing student work based on common rubrics
   D. Promoting conversation through purposeful and guided discussions about a book, piece of writing, or topic

Answer: B. Devoting 40% of instructional time to reading/writing
Only Answer B is an ineffective strategy. Recommendations are 50% and on a daily basis.

58. **Activities which focus on increasing fluency in academic reading include all of the following strategies except:**
(Average) (Skill 7.3)

   A. modeled reading
   B. repeated reading of a familiar text
   C. reading of signs, labels, and lists
   D. coached reading of appropriate materials

Answer: C. reading of signs, labels, and lists
Answers A, B, and D are appropriate for developing fluency. Only Answer C is of short, disconnected phrases that would probably not improve the reading of academic texts or literature.

59. **Fluency is based upon all of the following except:**
    (Rigorous) (Skill 7.3)

    A. a foundation of oral language skills
    B. familiarity with letter forms
    C. reading comprehension
    D. efficient decoding skills

Answer: C. reading comprehension
Reading instruction should include explicit instruction in A, B, and D to develop fluency. Answer C is a goal of reading instruction but not of fluency development skill.

60. **ESOL teaching encourages tasks that:**
    (Rigorous) (Skill 7.3)

    A. emphasize correct form
    B. give learners flexibility in problem solving
    C. encourage learners to concentrate on language use
    D. are demanding

Answer: B. give learners flexibility in problem solving
Answers A, C, and D are ineffective ESOL practice and are not recommended. Effective ESOL instruction gives the ELL many opportunities to show what he/she knows and understands. Thus, the correct choice is B.

61. **Which researcher is most associated with problem solving activities for language learning?**
    (Rigorous) (Skill 7.3)

    A. Gattegno
    B. Prabhu
    C. Wilkins
    D. Lewis

Answer: B. Prabhu
Option A. Gattegno was associated with the Silent Way. Option C. Wilkins developed the Notional/Functional Syllabus. Option D. Lewis proposed the idea of lexical chunks. The correct option is B. Prabhu who developed the idea of "gap" activities which include Reasoning and problem solving.

62. **A purpose of the "reading phase" is to:**
(Rigorous) (Skill 7.4)

A. establish a purpose
B. utilize background knowledge to study heading, chapter, and answer questions
C. use graphics to organize information
D. motivate the reader

Answer: B. utilize background knowledge to study heading, chapter, and answer questions
Answers A and D are pre-reading goals. Answer C is a post-reading strategy. Answer B is the correct choice, a reading phase strategy.

63. **When teaching initial literacy, teachers should focus on all of the following literacy skills except:**
(Average) (Skill 8.1)

A. culture
B. phonemic awareness
C. phonics
D. comprehension of different types of reading materials

Answer: A. culture
Answers B, C, and D are all important literacy skills. Answer A is not a literacy skill, but culture, especially the characteristics of the heritage language, may affect transfer of language skills to L2. Answer A is the correct choice.

64. **Which one of the following skills would probably have the most positive effect on developing literacy skills in ELLs?**
(Average) (Skill 8.2)

A. Oral storytelling traditions
B. Watching documentaries on TV
C. Visiting art museums
D. Attending concerts

Answer: A. Oral storytelling traditions
While all of the above could positively affect literacy development, the most probable would be Answer A. Oral storytelling encourages developing readers to follow a story line, look for the climax or main idea, and compare the written word to prior knowledge.

65. **Which of the following is a disadvantage to the instructor's of use of L1 in the L2 classroom or in L2 instruction?**
    (Rigorous) (Skill 8.2)

    A. Limits development of L2
    B. Reduces anxiety and fear
    C. Permits explanation of differences and similarities of L1 and L2
    D. Reduces time-consuming explanation of abstract concepts

Answer: A. Limits development of L2
Answer B, C, and D are positive aspects of the knowledge and use of L1 in the L2 classroom. Answer A is a disadvantage for some students who may become dependent on the use of L1 and not progress in L2.

66. **By acquiring knowledge of as few as _____ words, the ELL can understand _____ percent of an academic text.**
    (Rigorous) (Skill 8.3)

    A. 1000; 74
    B. 1500; 80
    C. 2000; 95
    D. 2500; 60

Answer: C. 2000; 95
The correct figures are 2000; 95—Answer C.

67. **Which one of the following word analysis skills is probably the most difficult for an ELL to learn?**
    (Average) (Skill 8.4)

    A. Prefixes and suffixes
    B. Sound-symbol correspondence
    C. Phonemic and morphemic awareness
    D. Cognates and false cognates

Answer: B. Sound-symbol correspondence
The elements of language mentioned in A, C, and D are present in other languages and these skills may be transferred to English. Answer B is the correct choice since English has many sounds for different letters.

68. **Which of the following activities is the most effective in learning to use the dictionary effectively?**
(Rigorous) (Skill 8.4)

A. Locating synonyms, phrases, and etymology of words
B. Looking up definitions and writing a sentence with the words
C. Rewriting the definition in your own words
D. Writing down the pronunciation guide and the definition

Answer: A. Locating synonyms, phrases, and etymology of words
According to Schumm, Options B, C, and D do not allow the learner to fully explore the parts of a dictionary and how to use it. Option A provides the student with additional information about the word and the range of information available in a dictionary. Option A is the best choice.

69. **Incorporating prior knowledge into L2 learning does not:**
(Average) (Skill 8.4)

A. permit readers to learn and remember more
B. cause poor readers
C. help readers to evaluate new arguments
D. improve comprehension

Answer: B. cause poor readers
Activating schema and incorporating previous knowledge into L2 learning will strengthen the learning process. It certainly does not cause poor readers.

70. **Which one of the following questions would be least effective in promoting critical-thinking skills when looking at a butterfly collection?**
(Rigorous) (Skill 8.4)

A. What are the parts of a butterfly?
B. What evidence do you find to support the idea...?
C. How would you classify a butterfly?
D. What colors are the butterflies?

Answer: D. What colors are the butterflies?
Questions that support critical-thinking skills are A, B, and C. Answer D asks about color and is the correct selection. A critical-thinking skill about the myriad of colors of butterflies could be, "Based on what you know, why do butterflies have so many different colors?"

71. **Which of the following is a meta-cognitive strategy?**
    (Average) (Skill 8.4)

    A. Practicing new language
    B. Summarizing long passages
    C. Skimming for necessary information
    D. Evaluating learning

Answer: D. Evaluating learning
Answers A, B, and C are cognitive strategies. Answer D is a meta-cognitive strategy.

72. **To analyze oral discourse, which of the following is not an analytical question?**
    (Rigorous) (Skill 8.4)

    A. How did you feel about the dialogue?
    B. How would you restate what the speaker said?
    C. How would people from your country act in a similar situation?
    D. Do you agree or disagree with what is said in the dialogue?

Answer: B. How would you restate what the speaker said?
Answers A, C, and D are all analytical questions. Answer B is a comprehension question and the correct selection.

73. **Which one of the following is not a purpose of informal reading assessment?**
    (Easy) (Skill 8.5)

    A. To gauge oral reading comprehension
    B. To assess vocabulary
    C. To assess fluency
    D. To assess silent reading comprehension

Answer: C. To assess fluency
Answers A, B, and D are all goals of informal reading assessments. Only Answer C is not; it is a goal of learning to read.

74. **Which one of the following is not a way to establish reliability when placing students with disabilities?**
    (Easy) (Skill 8.6)

    A. Using multiple raters
    B. Including multiple assessment measures
    C. Establishing clearly specified scoring criteria
    D. Using the Woodcock-Johnson III Diagnostic Reading Battery

Answer: D. Using the Woodcock-Johnson III Diagnostic Reading Battery
The Woodcock-Johnson III Diagnostic Reading Battery is widely used in formal reading assessments. While unquestionably reliable, it in itself does not establish reliability for placement of students with special needs.

75. **Which of the following is not a step in the Language Experience Approach?**
    (Average) (Skill 6.1)

    A. Students draw a picture to represent something personal about an experience
    B. Students dictate their story to the teacher
    C. The teacher reads the story revising where necessary
    D. The story is read in later days as a follow-up activity

Answer: C. The teacher reads the story revising where necessary
In the Language Experience Approach, the teacher writes the revised sentences on the storyboard making the necessary corrections at this time.

76. **Which one of the following is not a way to encourage non-graded writing practice?**
    (Easy) (Skill 9.1)

    A. Writing a dialog in pairs
    B. Rewriting a passage or summary in the ELL's own words
    C. Writing from the perspective of another
    D. Writing a summary to hand in

Answer: D. Writing a summary to hand in
Answers A, B, and C are ways students can practice writing without a teacher's evaluation. A summary to be handed-in suggests evaluation even if it is informal.

77. **The purpose of frontloading vocabulary is:**
(Average) (Skill 9.1)

A. vocabulary development
B. increase reading comprehension
C. explaining content
D. increasing spelling proficiency

Answer: B. increase reading comprehension
All of the answers are interrelated and valuable instructional goals. Nevertheless, the main goal is B, increasing reading comprehension.

78. **Reid (1987) divides the writing process into two broad divisions. They are:**
(Average) (Skill 9.2)

A. composing; pre-writing
B. pre-writing; drafting
C. brainstorming; drafting
D. composition; revision

Answer: D. composition; revision
Only Answer D considers the revision process which is an integral part of the writing process, and thus, the correct choice.

79. **Which one of the following writing activities is not appropriate for different proficiency levels?**
(Average) (Skill 9.3)

A. Reading and writing letters to pen pals
B. Creating exhibits or projects
C. Traditional book reports
D. Organizing lists

Answer: C. Traditional book reports
ELLs should work on purposeful, authentic writing activities. Answer A, B, and D are authentic tasks. Answer C is not. It is an artificial construct for the purposes of schooling.

80. **Which one of the following is not an appropriate activity for engaging ELLs in real-life communicative activities?**
(Average) (Skill 9.3)

A. Oral discussion based on a news story
B. Researching an assigned topic and reporting back to peers
C. Reporting on a new video game
D. Discussing a movie with a friend

Answer: B. Researching an assigned topic and reporting back to peers
Answers A, C, and D are authentic because they are engaging the learner in an activity they are interested in and are authentic. Research on assigned topics is not authentic and frequently uninteresting to students. The correct answer is B.

81. **Emerging ELLs need instruction in conventions of written Standard English such as:**
(Average) (Skill 9.4)

A. syntax
B. discourse
C. vocabulary
D. types of written texts

Answer: A. syntax
Answers B, C, and D are not conventions. Answer B is a type of connected speech or writing, Answer C is necessary to write well, and Answer D refers to genres and other types of texts. Only Answer A—syntax—refers to a convention of written Standard English.

82. **Which one of the following is not a valid purpose of assessment?**
(Rigorous) (Skill 9.5)

A. Determining a student's potential
B. Determination of a student's present academic performance level
C. Eligibility for a program
D. Diagnosis of special learner disabilities

Answer: A. Determining a student's potential
Answers B, C, and D are all valid purposes of assessment. Answer A is a factor that tests, specifically I.Q. tests, are unable to define.

83. **Tests which evaluate an individual as compared to others are:**
(Easy) (Skill 9.5)

A. standardized
B. authentic
C. norm referenced
D. criterion referenced

Answer: C. norm referenced
Answer D may be discarded as criterion referenced tests evaluate an individual's knowledge of specific content. Answer A might be true, but standardized tests may be criterion referenced. Answer B concerns tests being relevant to a student's life, and not necessarily comparing the student to others. Only Answer C is specifically designed to compare one individual with others.

84. **Which of the following tests is used to refine specific learning disabilities?**
(Rigorous) (Skill 9.5)

A. Wechsler Intelligence Scale for Children
B. Sanford-Binet IV
C. Gardner's multiple intelligence tests
D. Kaufman Assessment Batter for Children

Answer: C. Gardner's multiple intelligence tests
Answers A, B, and D are used to predict school performance. Recent research into multiple intelligences has helped identify specific learning disabilities shown by significant discrepancies between scores on different intelligences. Answer C is the correct answer.

85. **Which one of the following goals will not be discovered through assessment?**
(Rigorous) (Skill 9.5)

A. If student is ready for new information
B. Strategies for improving programs
C. If student is lacking prerequisite skills
D. Program weaknesses

Answer: B. Strategies for improving programs
Answers A, C, and D may all be discovered through assessment. Answer B, strategies for improving programs, are not revealed through assessment. These are the result of analysis of the information discovered through assessment, and the teacher's knowledge of alternative strategies for teaching his/her charges.

86.   **Which of the following writing assessments uses holistic scoring?**
       (Rigorous) (Skill 9.5)

       A. International English Language Test System (IELTS)
       B. National Assessment of Educational Progress (NAEP)
       C. Test of English as a Foreign Language (TOEFL)
       D. Michigan Writing Assessment

Answer: C. Test of English as a Foreign Language (TOEFL)
Answer A (IELTS) and D (Michigan Writing Assessment) use analytic scoring.
Answer B (NAEP) uses trait scoring. Only C (TOEFL) uses holistic scoring.

87.   **Which one of the following is a disadvantage of portfolio assessment?**
       (Average) (Skill 9.5)

       A. They are integrative
       B. They produce variable samples
       C. They are motivating
       D. They are formative

Answer: B. They produce variable samples
Answers A, C, and D are all advantages of portfolio assessment. The disadvantage
is they are produce variable samples; some tasks may elicit better writing because
they are more interesting. The correct answer is B.

88.   **Arreaga-Mayer (1998) suggests all of the following constructs for
       successful ELLs except:**
       (Rigorous) (Skill 10.1)

       A. collaborative/cooperative learning
       B. input slightly above competence level
       C. involvement
       D. mediation/feedback

Answer: B. input slightly above competence level
Answers A, C, and D are constructs put forth by Arreaga-Mayer, except B which
Krashen theorized. Krashen stated his formula as i+ 1.

89. **Which one of the following is not one of the four basic components of peer tutoring?**
(Average) (Skill 10.1)

A. Weekly competing teams
B. Highly structured teaching procedures
C. Daily, public postings of individual and team scores
D. Building on prior knowledge

Answer: D. Building on prior knowledge
Answers A, B, and C are basic components of peer tutoring. Answer D, activating prior knowledge, is a basic ESOL practice, but not a specific component of peer tutoring.

90. **All of the following are integrated approaches to language teaching except:**
(Average) (Skill 10.1)

A. Language Experience Approach
B. cooperative learning
C. task-based or experiential learning
D. graphic organizers

Answer: A. Language Experience Approach
Answers B, C, and D are integrated approaches to language teaching. Answer A: LEA, targets vocabulary and reading development by building on prior knowledge.

91. **Graphic organizers provide students with:**
(Average) (Skill 10.1)

A. projects to carry out
B. a means for organizing information
C. negotiated meaning
D. cooperative incentivizes

Answer: B. a means for organizing information
Answer A is a component of task-based learning. Answer C is a benefit of cooperative learning. Answer D is an element of peer-mediated instruction. Thus, Answer B is the correct choice as graphic organizers help students organize information.

92. **According to Chomsky's Universal Grammar (UG) and Language Acquisition Device (LAD) theories, younger learners have less difficulty learning language because:**
    (Rigorous) (Skill 10.3)

    A. language is controlled by external factors
    B. after puberty, the critical period shuts down
    C. their LAD is still active
    D. language abilities increase with age

Answer: C. their LAD is still active
Answer A is based on Piaget's theory of language as controlled by external information and social interaction. Answer B is based upon the work of Krashen and Felix who both proposed theories for the close of the L2 critical period at puberty. Answer D is based on the research of Newport & Supalla supporting Piaget's theory. Only Answer C is part of Chomsky's theory of L2 development.

93. **All of the following are advantages of learning and using more than one language except:**
    (Rigorous) (Skill 10. 3)

    A. increases visual-social abilities
    B. supports cognitive flexibility
    C. limits problem solving abilities
    D. allows increased understanding of concepts

Answer: C. limits problem solving abilities
Only Answer C is untrue of L2 advantages.

94. **All of the following are true about the Massachusetts Comprehensive Assessment System (MCAS) except:**
(*Rigorous*) *(Skill 10.4)*

A. Each public school student in the state is tested in grades 3-8 and once in high school in English.
B. The Massachusetts Curriculum Frameworks forms the basis of the test battery.
C. Each public school student in the state is tested in grades 3-8 and once in high school in mathematics.
D. Each public school student in the state is tested in grades 3-8 and once in high school in computer science.

Answer: D. Each public school student in the state is tested in grades 3-8 and once in high school in computer science.
Answers A, B, and C are true of the MCAS test battery. Students are required to take a science and engineering/technology test once in elementary, middle, and high school. Answer D is the correct choice.

95. **To distinguish between ELLs and ELLs with disabilities, which one of the following testing procedures is not recommended?**
(*Average*) *(Skill 10.4)*

A. Intelligence quotient (IQ) test
B. Criterion-referenced assessments
C. Curriculum-referenced assessments
D. Observations from school, home, and community

Answer: A. Intelligence quotient (IQ) test
Answers B, C, and D are effective procedures for determining placement for ELLs with disabilities. IQ tests are not recommended as they are frequently culturally biased. If used, they should be used in careful conjunction with more representative test types. Answer A is the correct choice.

96. When considering students with behavioral disabilities, teachers are most concerned about behaviors which are:
(Rigorous) (Skill 10.4)

A. sporadic
B. intense
C. short-lived
D. infrequent

Answer: B. intense
While all behaviors which disrupt the established classroom norms are of concern, Answer B is the most significant in identifying possible behavioral problems and the correct choice.

97. Teacher Assistance Teams (TATS) should be composed of all of the following except the:
(Average) (Skill 10.4)

A. school administrators
B. guidance counselors
C. media specialists
D. parent(s)

Answer: C. media specialists
Answer A, B, and D may all be members of a TAT. Media specialists could be consulted for additional materials that would help in special education cases, but would not form part of the normal TAT. Answer C is the correct choice.

98. When considering referrals for specialized services, all of the following are considered except:
(Rigorous) (Skill 10.4)

A. student characteristics
B. parents' request for/against referral
C. multidisciplinary evaluation
D. institutional factors

Answer: C. multidisciplinary evaluation
Answer A, B and D are all considered when evaluation of a student is requested by a teacher, parent, or other person. Answer C occurs after the referral. It is the next step in the lengthy process of establishing special services.

99. **To protect students from inequities in the referral process, federal law explicitly provides for:**
   (Rigorous) (Skill 10.4)

   A. non-discriminatory evaluation procedures
   B. an independent education evaluation
   C. a multidisciplinary team using several pieces of information to formulate a referral
   D. testing of the child in L1 unless clearly not feasible to do so

Answer: B. an independent education evaluation
Answers A, C, and D are all mandated by federal law. Answer B is an alternative that may be permitted when the parents feel the school's evaluation was inappropriate, but it is not mandated.

100. **Information for placing students with learning or behavioral disabilities will usually include all of the following except:**
   (Rigorous) (Skill 10.4)

   A. past academic performance
   B. neurological reports
   C. notes from auxiliary/substitute teachers
   D. speech and language evaluations

Answer: C. notes from auxiliary/substitute teachers
Answers A, B, and D are all important elements of the documentation needed for referral. Answer C, notes from auxiliary/substitute teachers, should not be dismissed out-of-hand, but followed-up on as a more formal, written report which details the observations, before this document is included in the student's file. Therefore, Answer C is the correct option.

CPSIA information can be obtained at www.ICGtesting.com
Printed in the USA
BVOW10s2345060116

432017BV00005B/68/P

9 781607 870845